WELLINGTON'S FO

The East Coast of Spain 1810 – 1814

Nick Lipscombe

Limited Edition Version

(No. 193 of 750)

Tarragona and Fort Olivo

This is the first in a series of books to be published on the Napoleonic Wars by Gerrard Books. For details of how to obtain further copies of this book see: www.nick-lipscombe.net

Published By
Gerrard Books
PO Box 112
Rochester, Kent.
ME1 2EX

Printed By
S. R. Print Design
Partida Murtar 2/2 Bajo
03750 Pedreguer, Alicante.
Spain

CONTENTS

Acknowledgements

I am indebted to Ian Fletcher for his agreement to establish (bilaterally) Gerrard Books; to José Luis Arcón Dominguez for his continued help and encyclopaedic knowledge of (in particular) events on the East Coast of Spain; to Peter Harrington, the curator of the Anne S. K. Brown Military Collection, for providing the two prints; to the Ayuntamiento at Castalla for allowing me to publish the copy of Langlois' painting; and to Sarah and Robin King for their indefatigable support in reading and re-reading my text and offering 'suggestions'. Thank you all.

1810

11 April - 13 May	Siege of Lérida.
15 May – 5 June	Siege of Mequinenza.
16 December	Siege of Tortosa commences.

1811

2 January	Siege of Tortosa concluded.
4 May – 28 June	Siege of Tarragona.
19 September – 11 October	Siege of Oropesa.
23 September – 26 October	Siege of Saguntum.
25 October	Battle of Saguntum.
28 December	Siege of Valencia commences.

1812

9 January	Siege of Valencia concluded.
20 January – 2 February	Siege of Peñiscola.
21 July	First Battle of Castalla.
31 July	Maitland & Expeditionary Force arrives off the Catalan coast.

1813

11 April	Combat at Yecla.
12 April	Combat at Biar.
13 April	Second Battle of Castalla.
3 – 15 June	Failed Allied Siege of Tarragona.
30 July – 15 August	Allied Blockade of Tarragona.
13 September	Combat at Ordal.

1814

16 April	Sortie from Barcelona.

Peñiscola Castle

By July 1807 Napoleon was master of continental Europe and in an incontestably commanding position. The Austrians had been defeated at Ulm and Austerlitz in 1805 and effectively neutralised; the Prussians had been defeated at Jena and Auerstadt in 1806 and dismembered; and the Russians, after a bloody draw at Eylau, were defeated at Friedland in 1807 and humbled. The Fourth Coalition lay in tatters and Napoleon was at the acme of his providence and yet, despite his triumphs, one prize still eluded him. His fanatical obsession with the Great Invasion, and consequent subjugation of Britain had suffered an irreparable setback off Cape Trafalgar in 1805. The range and reach of Britain's amphibian power and her emergent commerce infuriated Napoleon and thwarted his plans both in Europe and worldwide. The elimination of the Danish Fleet in 1807 rendered any aspiration to engage the British at sea untenable and left an attack on her trade the best way to compel Britain to petition for peace. Napoleon's Continental System would lead to a boycott of British trade, bring the nation to its knees and, through economic necessity, coerce Britain to the negotiating table; perceivably, it could also bring about revolutionary change through the bellies of the poor.

Napoleonic diktats, known as the Berlin Decrees, had already been issued in 1806 and the French wasted little time in reinforcing their intentions upon the compliant crowned heads of Europe. By 1808 all of Europe, except Sweden and Portugal, were in a state of enforced hostility towards Britain and, while the latter made an attempt to counter the blockade, the fact remained that Britain's trade fell off at an alarming rate. Corrupt French officials however were able to issue trading licences and this loophole was capitalised upon by, in particular, the Iberian nations. The ink was hardly dry on the peace treaty with Russia, following the meeting at Tilsit in July 1807, before Napoleon's gaze fell upon his southern neighbours. Spanish duplicity had begun to manifest itself as early as 1806 when the Spanish First Minister Manuel Godoy issued an ill-judged proclamation clearly aimed against France. Ostensibly Napoleon maintained friendly relations with Spain but he began to mass more troops along the Pyrenees; Portugal was a more immediate concern and he needed Spanish compliance to instigate the first part of his plan.

The Treaty of Fontainebleau drawn up between France and Spain was, in the main, forced on the latter allowing French troops to transit Spain in order to invade and subjugate Portugal, after which the ill fated nation would be partitioned and the spoils distributed. However, before the ink was dry and the Treaty fully ratified, the first elements of the (so called) First Corps of Observation of the Gironde under the command of General Jean Andoche Junot had crossed the Pyrenees and headed west. Within six weeks Portugal had capitulated and, in the nick of time, the Portuguese regency and royal court had executed a well prepared contingency plan and fled to Brazil. The apparent ease with which this national conquest had been achieved prompted Napoleon to consider that the conquest of Spain would be a similarly straightforward affair. In so doing he underestimated the tenacity of the Spanish people, the power of the Catholic Church and the military challenges of subjugation; he also overestimated the wealth and global influence of Spain's empirical roots. Within months many more troops had crossed into Spain and some under the command of General Philibert Duhesme had crossed into Catalonia; the pretence was over and Napoleon was locked in a struggle that was to ebb and flow for the next six years.

Napoleon's long term strategy in the Peninsula may have succeeded had he chosen to manipulate the Spanish Bourbon king rather than replace him with his elder brother Joseph Bonaparte. There were many in Spain who had tired of the *ancien régime* and desired change but not under the jackboot of foreign subjugation. The backlash, when it finally came in Madrid on 2 May 1808, was more rebellion than revolution but it was enough to create the catalyst for a slow burning national revolt which triggered the Spanish War of Independence (La Guerra de la Independencia). The repercussions of Spanish rebellion and ensuing conflict were felt across the border in Portugal but with its military largely dismantled, following Junot's invasion, their options were limited. Nevertheless, with Junot's 26,000 men tied down in a nation with 90,000 square kilometres and with a 1,300 kilometre long coastline, the opportunities for foreign military intervention were ripe. Britain, with its unchallengeable naval strength and undeniable thirst for a military success on the European mainland, found the proposition of involvement in the Peninsula an ideal platform from which to open a second front, tie down large numbers of French troops, deny Bonaparte the naval resources of Spain and Portugal (ships and ports), discredit French claims to and aspirations in Spain's and Portugal's New World colonies and, perhaps most importantly, provide the nation an opportunity to take the fight to Napoleon on a scale that, at the time, was not feasible elsewhere.

British intervention in Portugal in August 1808 led to a quick and decisive victory for the British and the liberation of the nation. Only a month earlier a French corps under General Pierre Dupont had been beaten by a Spanish army at Bailén; with the French naval squadron captured in the Bay of Cádiz, the siege of Saragossa not progressing according to plan and the failed attempts to capture Valencia, Gerona and Rosas, the French commanders had much to lament. Within months, however, Napoleon arrived in the Iberian theatre at the head of an additional 130,000 reinforcements and quickly turned the tide. The combined Spanish armies were comprehensively beaten at Espinosa de Los Monteros, Burgos o de Gamonal and Tudela; Madrid was re-captured and the British army, under the command of Lieutenant General Sir John Moore, was driven to the Galician coast and into the waiting naval transports. Napoleon considered his demonstration complete and, having left clear instructions to his subordinates as to how to bring the Spanish nation to heel, he departed the theatre never to return.

In the immediate aftermath of Moore's harrowing retreat and his death on the field of battle at the Galician port of La Coruña, the likelihood of a British 'return' was doubtful. Lieutenant General Sir Arthur Wellesley, the commander and architect of Britain's military success in defeating Junot in Portugal the year prior, maintained that Portugal could continue to be defended by a force of 30,000 men and would, in the process, tie-down at least three times that number of French soldiers. His proposals, supported by Lord Castlereagh the Secretary for War, were endorsed by Prime Minister Portland's Cabinet and within weeks another British force had been despatched. For a second time Portugal was liberated and the subsequent link-up with the Spanish Army of Estremadura resulted in a hard fought victory at Talavera in July 1809. Any optimism was, however, quickly dispelled as three French corps moved in support of Marshal Claude Victor's and General Horace-François Sebastiani's defeated forces and the defence of King Joseph and the Spanish capital. Viscount Wellington, as Wellesley became following the allied victory at Talavera, withdrew with his small British force to the Portuguese border. Within weeks, the catastrophic defeats suffered by the Spanish during the disastrous Autumn Campaign coupled with Napoleon's resounding victories over the Austrians and the corresponding collapse of the Fifth Coalition, drove

Wellington deep into Portugal. It was to be a long winter but Wellington used the time to train and reequip the Portuguese Army; from 1810 onwards it was an Anglo-Portuguese force, remaining so until the end of the war.

By 1810 Napoleon's objectives in Iberia had carved two strategic axes of advance and corresponding lines of communication, the first from Bayonne to Madrid and on to Lisbon, the second from Bayonne to Madrid and south to Cádiz and Gibraltar. The former axis placed the *Grande Armée* on a collision course with the newly fashioned Anglo-Portuguese Army under Wellington. The latter axis resulted in more of an allied collaborative defence protecting Spain's executive holed-up at Cádiz, and Britain's maritime and trading interests at Gibraltar. Two additional struggles were playing out on either side of these axes; the first was in the north of the country and along the Cantabrian coast, the second was in Catalonia and along the Mediterranean east coast.

Britain's involvement in these two regional struggles was, in the main, restricted to Royal Navy support and sea-denial patrolling. However, it was that very sea supremacy, coupled with the extant road network and the absence of any French troops in the east coast region, which enabled Spain to utilise, unhindered, the Mediterranean ports of Tarragona, Valencia, Alicante and Cartagena as logistic hubs supplying the Spanish armies and her people. Napoleon cited this as one of the principal reasons for the *Grande Armée's*

failure to subdue the population, decisively defeat the Spanish armies and to drive the troublesome British from Iberia. Accordingly, in late 1810, he issued orders to General Luis Gabriel Suchet to commence operations and capture the three key cities and ports. The battle for the East Coast had begun.

The East Coast Theatre of Operations 1810 – 1813 (Suchet's Memoirs)

Suchet had commanded the 1st Division within the 5th Corps at Jena and deployed with it to Iberia in the autumn 1808 before being given command of the 3rd Corps, succeeding Junot in April 1809. The chain of command for this Corps was to change from Madrid to Paris in the early part of 1810, but not before Marshal Nicolas Soult, the Duke of Dalmatia, had ordered Suchet to attempt to capture Valencia by a *coup de main* in concert with his planned invasion of Andalusia. Suchet's attempt failed and, on return to Saragossa, he received a sharp Napoleonic rebuke for having undertaken the operation. Unequivocal guidelines accompanied the censure. The 'Army of Aragón' as Suchet's new command was titled, was subordinated to Paris alone and future operations were to be conducted in concert with the French Army in Catalonia.

Suchet's first task was to capture the fort at Lérida. He commenced the siege in mid May and within a month the fort was in French hands; it was a promising start.

Luis Gabriel SUCHET
(Bonaparte's Memoirs ~ Fauvelet de Bourrienne)

The capture of Lérida opened up communications between Aragón and Catalonia; before linking up with the French Army of Catalonia, however,

Suchet elected to capture the fort at Mequinenza in order to secure his rearward lines of communication with his base and headquarters at Saragossa. A brigade had been sent to invest the structure on 15 May, but the French engineers were required to build a road to enable the siege guns to get sufficiently close. By 1 June the road was complete and the fort was taken four days later. Suchet now controlled all the key points within Aragón, but the concentration of his forces to achieve this advantageous position had enabled the Spanish *guerrilleros* to regroup and recommence operations. The French commander was thereby forced to turn his attention back to dealing with this resurgent threat.

The Fort of Mequinenza on the north bank of the River Ebro (Belmas)

Napoleon was delighted at Suchet's success, which contrasted starkly with the other rather dismal reports from across the Iberian theatre. Capitalising on Suchet's achievements he penned instructions for the invasion of the Kingdom of Valencia and, in the first phase, the capture of the Kingdom's capital city and port. The scheme was to commence with preliminary operations against Tortosa and Tarragona, thereby securing north-south communications with France and the French armies of Catalonia and Aragón. Both commanders had hoped to receive some support from the new 9th Corps, which had assembled at Bayonne at the start of the year. They were, however, to be disappointed as this formation, created by Napoleon's directive that all regiments in Spain were to establish a 4th battalion, headed south-west in mid 1810 to support Marshal André Masséna's (Prince of Essling) new Army of Portugal. In concert with

Suchet's operations from the north, Soult was also tasked to move against Cartagena from the west but, due to a combination of Soult's intransigence and an outbreak of yellow fever in Murcia, this parallel operation did not commence until December 1811.

Napoleon considered the capture of Tortosa vital, despite the city not lying directly on the north-south coastal line of communication, as it possessed the only bridge across the River Ebro in the immediate area (there was only a ferry at Amposta). Furthermore, it was the only city which stored sufficient resources for an army on the march. The old medieval walls enclosed the inhabited part and a number of outer works had been constructed following the Spanish Wars of Succession in 1708. It was defended by a very strong garrison of over 7,000 men and 182 guns but the Spanish governor, General Miguel Lilli, Conde de Alacha, proved to be a most unreliable inspiration to the defenders.

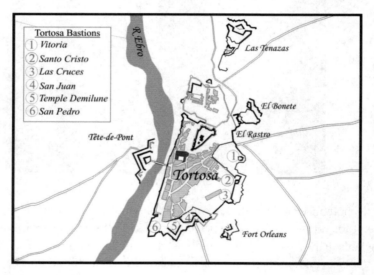

Marshal Etienne Macdonald, commanding the French Army of Catalonia, was tasked to provide protection to Suchet's northern flank, while General Louis François Musnier's Division was sent south to counter any approach made by the Valencian Army. It was not an easy operation; the movement of the siege train and equipment took an inordinate amount of time. The roads were appalling and Suchet was forced to move the 52 guns on specially constructed boats down the Ebro. The low levels of water in the river delayed the scheme in August and September; then in October, when matters appeared to be improving for the French, Macdonald was compelled to lift his flanking force and return north to restore order against a growing insurgent movement that was threatening the French garrisons at both Barcelona and Gerona. Macdonald had stabilised the situation by early December and was back on the lower Ebro on 13 December; Suchet wasted no time in establishing the cordon, which was in-place three days later. Four hastily constructed bridges were established above and below the town to transport the heavy guns and engineer stores from the west to the east bank. Following consultation with his chief engineer, General François Haxo, and his chief of artillery, General Sylvain Valée, Suchet elected to attack from the south against the San Pedro Bastion and undertake an operation to neutralise the guns in Fort Orleans, as the latter covered the approaches to the former (See Map 1). The soil in the valley yielded easily to the pioneers' shovels and the attackers were able to make rapid progress, much to the consternation of the on looking garrison.

The first parallel was complete by Christmas Day and work commenced immediately on the saps. However, the digging at Fort Orleans was less straightforward and Suchet was forced to deploy miners to hack out the bedrock. Lilli, alarmed at French progress, ordered a major sortie on 28 December, with 3,000 men attacking the French opposite Fort Orleans while another large group attacked the main breaching batteries. The former attack failed as the Spanish did not press home their numerical advantage, allowing General Pierre Habert to fall upon them with the 5e Léger and 11e Ligne and drive them back into the town. However, the other group managed to gain access to the lower parallel and caused considerable damage before being beaten back by the 44e Ligne. The French spent much of the following day repairing the destruction but on 29 December they opened with forty five guns. The bastions guns in Fort Orleans and San Juan were quickly neutralised and the bridge of boats was all but destroyed. The Spanish abandoned the tête-du-pont the next day. The French pressed forward and work began on a third parallel, with the aim of mining the scarp of the San Pedro Bastion. By 31 December the attackers had placed four 24-pounder guns within twenty-five metres of the walls and the next day the governor raised the white flag. Lilli's initial terms were entirely unacceptable to Suchet and when he resumed the attack on 2 January, blasting a practicable breach, a second white flag appeared within minutes. Initial parley seemed inconclusive but Suchet then marched to the gate and bullied the aged governor into submission. After only eighteen days, Tortosa was in French hands.

'After two years, the 7ᵗʰ Corps found itself deeply embroiled in a difficult war in Catalonia; the belligerent character of the inhabitants, the nature of the country, mountainous, cut with ravines and defiles, allowed the Spanish to dominate the French lines of communication, and harass the French on the march, forcing them to supply large troop escorts to all their convoys'. So wrote the French historian Jacques Belmas in 1837 in his journal on the French sieges of the war. Macdonald would undoubtedly have agreed with this statement and added that he also had to garrison a number of forts and fortified towns as well as fend off the regular Spanish Army of Catalonia. His reaction, therefore, to Napoleon's decree of 10 March 1811 would have been one of anger and amazement. The Emperor, keen to reinforce Suchet's early success, stripped Macdonald of the provinces Lérida, Tarragona and Tortosa and handed these, along with 18,000 men from Macdonald's force, to Suchet's Army of Aragón.

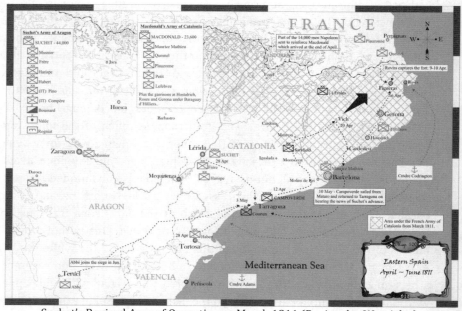

Suchet's Revised Area of Operations – March 1811 (Peninsular War Atlas)

Suchet now had 43,000 men but his area of responsibility included his original area of Aragón and incorporated half of Catalonia, north of the Ebro. Napoleon's plan for the next phase of the subjugation of the East Coast required Suchet to capture the vital city and port of Tarragona; for this operation Suchet was expected to provide both the besieging and covering force. Musnier and Major General Marie Paris were left to defend Aragón from Mina's guerrillas, while Habert and Major General Louis Abbé were deployed to Tortosa and Teruel respectively, to guard against any northerly movement by the Valencians. The balance of 20,000 men were to march by two routes; the majority from Lérida while Habert moved north with the siege train from Tortosa. In fact, General Luis González, Marques de Campoverde had missed an excellent opportunity to venture south, with his not inconsiderable Spanish Army of Catalonia, and intercept Habert and destroy these siege guns en route. However, the Spanish were soon to revel in an even greater success: even before Suchet had commenced the advance towards Tarragona he received the astonishing news that the Spanish irregulars had captured the significant fortress at Figueras.

Macdonald wrote to Suchet, imploring him to return the former 7th Corps troops. 'My dear general, in the name of public welfare, the service of the emperor requires imperatively and without delay, the most speedy succour, otherwise upper Catalonia is lost'. Suchet was not so sure; the information regarding Figueras had taken twelve days to reach him and it would take the same amount of time to gather the dispersed 7th Corps units and return them. Already the numbers of defenders within the fort had increased to 3,000 and on 16 April additional regular troops arrived from Baron Eroles' Division, which was operating to the west. Suchet elected to continue with his preparations for the siege at Tarragona, confident his decision would meet with Napoleon's approval.

On 3 May Suchet's force approached Tarragona and the advance guard drove in the Spanish outposts west of the Francoli River. The next day, operations continued on the east bank aimed to rid the area of Spanish troops and cut and hold the road north to Valls. However, Admiral Edward Codrington's combined fleet of Anglo-Spanish gunboats prevented the French encroaching too close to the town and shoreline to the east and west. Furthermore, a squadron of Codrington's frigates also harried and delayed Habert's unwieldy siege train column as it lumbered north along the exposed coast road from Tortosa. In the interim the French strengthened the cordon and the engineer and artillery commanders (Rogniat and Valée) conducted their reconnaissance, concluding that an attack from the west was the most practical. Campoverde (having moved to relieve Figueras) had returned to the city by sea on 10 May. With the garrison strength increased to 10,000, they immediately commenced sorties against the besiegers.

Sylvain Charles VALÉE   Pierre Joseph HABERT   Isidore HARISPE

The French siege train consisted of 66 siege guns including twenty-four of the heavy 24-pounder guns and eighteen heavy mortars. Before construction of trenches and parallels could commence, Suchet needed to drive-off the allied ships to prevent their fire hindering the building of siege works. Accordingly, a large redoubt was erected at the mouth of the Francoli River on the west bank (opposite Fort Francoli) and, on 13 May, it was armed with guns and mortars. The ships' guns were unable to productively respond and the fleet was forced to withdraw, allowing work on the first parallel to begin in earnest on 16 May.

At about this time Rogniat and Valée informed Suchet that the siege works were going to take about ten days to complete and, *pro tem*, Suchet decided to attempt the capture of Fort Olivo. The liberation of this structure was necessary as it enfiladed the French batteries and dominated the north-western parts of the lower suburbs and main city (See Map 2). Between 22 and 28 May, work commenced on three battery positions, but the engineers remained dubious about their ability to blast practicable breaches in the Fort as the walls were carved out of solid rock. They also noted that the rear (i.e. south) of the structure offered more promising opportunities. Accordingly, Suchet decided to try to capture the structure by escalade on the night of 29 May. The attack was delivered and quite by chance, as the assaulting troops made their way south, they came upon the Spanish battalion which was transiting from the city to relieve the guard in the outlying fort. The two groups of infantry were locked in chaotic hand-to-hand fighting and, in the darkness, some of the attackers gained entry to the Olivo Fort. This group, albeit small, was able to destroy a gate enabling the balance of the French infantry to enter. By morning, despite a determined counter attack by the Spanish, the Fort was in French hands. Campoverde immediately ordered all the guns on the north side of the Tarragona to bombard the place, but the French burrowed down and held on; they needed only to deny the feature to the defenders.

Map of the French Siege of Tarragona - See also Map 2

The next day Campoverde convened a council of war and informed the garrison that the only way to defeat Suchet was to attack his lines of communication and to fall upon his rear. He then promptly departed by sea in an attempt to galvanise the *somatenes* (Catalan home guard) and gather the remnants of Eroles' and General Pedro Sarsfield's divisions to act as the nucleus for this force. With General José Caro, the original governor, already deployed south in a similar mission (to rouse support from the Army of Valencia) command fell to General Juan Senen Contreras.

On 1 June the French batteries began bombarding the Fort Francoli and the San Carlos' and Orleans' bastions and, during the night of 7 June, Contreras ordered the Spanish defenders in the Fort to withdraw and abandon the structure. It was a grave mistake to give up this stronghold without a fight; with the structure in French hands, they could work unhindered on the second parallel. By 16 June the new batteries in this forward line were ready to open. Despite two sorties on the nights of 11 and 14 June the attackers were making steady progress and on the night of 16 June the Prince's Lunette was taken by assault. The defenders' position was now increasingly ominous and Contreras sent pleas for help to Campoverde who had, by now, been 'absent' for three weeks. There was a glimmer of hope later the same day with news that General José Miranda's Division had departed north from Valencia with an additional 11,000 men. In the end, however, Miranda did not venture too far north and satisfied himself with cutting the French lines of communication to the Ebro valley. Suchet, unperturbed, did not react; his target was in sight.

At 7 p.m. on 21 June the lower town was stormed by five columns of massed grenadier and *voltigeur* companies, through the breaches in the San Carlos' and Orleans' bastions. Both these attacks were successful and by the morning the French had control of the lower town and harbour. Work began immediately on a third parallel within this newly acquired zone. Meanwhile, Campoverde had resolved to attack, but the outlying French cavalry piquets provided early warning of their advance and the attack was beaten off with ease. News of a British expeditionary force despatched from Gibraltar, consisting of 1,200 men under Colonel John Skerrett, encouraged Campoverde to request their help. Skerrett and Commodore Codrington landed on 26 June to assess the situation. Skerrett had clear orders from General Thomas Graham (Lord Lynedoch, the Commander of British Forces at Cadiz) not to land his troops if he considered the town a lost cause. Both Skerrett and Codrington had reservations and these were confirmed when Campoverde allocated Skerrett's force the mission of keeping open the lines of retreat north of the city. Not surprisingly, they elected not to land the British infantry, causing deep resentment and a corresponding worsening of morale among the defenders.

It was of little consequence; on 27 June twenty-two breaching guns opened at dawn and at five that evening, the assault was made. Following a night of street fighting, and associated atrocities, the town was in French hands. News of this uncompromising treatment was, subsequently, to have a significant effect upon the inhabitants of Valencia during the siege of that city prompting their surrender. Suchet recalled, *'We took nearly ten thousand men and twenty pair of colours; including the guns in the Olivo and the lower town, we were in possession of three hundred and thirty-seven pieces of ordnance, fifteen thousand muskets, one hundred and fifty thousand weight of powder, forty thousand cannon-balls and bombs and four millions of cartridges'.*

Street fighting on the steps of Tarragona Cathedral (Thiers)

Along with the walls of Tarragona crumbled Campoverde's reputation; he held a council of war on 1 July and elected to abandon Catalonia altogether. Sarsfield was furious and Codrington refused to sanction the findings of the council or to transport the Catalan forces; he consented only to repatriate Miranda to Valencia.

Suchet meanwhile was repairing the walls and defences of his latest conquest. The capture of which was to earn him his Marshal's baton; indeed, he was the only one of Napoleon's generals to earn this ultimate promotion in the Peninsula. He made contact with General David Maurice Mathieu (the governor) at Barcelona and established a plan to re-open communications with Macdonald, who had remained motionless on the outskirts of Figueras. Suchet realised he would now have to help his colleague and moved north, at the head of Harispe's and Frère's divisions, which arrived at Vich on 15 July. He immediately despatched flying columns to determine the whereabouts of the French and Spanish forces in the area. Macdonald, once located, was clearly in control of the situation and both commanders anticipated that he would be able to re-establish control in northern Catalonia once Figueras capitulated, which was just a matter of days.

Suchet headed back south to open lines of communication between Barcelona and Lérida and, in so doing, was required to capture the precipitous Montserrat, the site of 'Our Lady of Montserrat', a renaissance church and large monastery. There were no fortifications on top of the steep rocky feature, but two batteries covered the main approach road and the buildings and walls of the monastery had been loopholed. On 25 July Abbé's Brigade made the assault with five battalions and met stiff resistance from the Spanish gunners who stood by their colours to the last. However, with the guns finally silenced, Abbé was preparing his men for the final assault when the defenders started streaming from the complex. The skirmishers sent to the rear of the hill had found access, collected three hundred men and delivered a surprise attack from that direction. Our Lady of Montserrat had fallen and with it the invincibility of this holy edifice. Suchet was now able to spend the next few months securing his gains in Catalonia, and strengthen those areas under his responsibility, before embarking on the next phase of the subjugation of the East Coast – the prized city and port of Valencia.

The Tarragona Plaque to the Heroes of the 1811 Siege

In July, the Regency had appointed Captain General Joaquín Blake y Joyes to assume overall command of the Spanish armies of Valencia and Murcia in an attempt to thwart French success in the region. Blake was of émigré Irish parentage, born in Malaga in 1759, he was one of the best Spanish commanders of the war. He was also one of the most unlucky. He had fought and beaten Suchet at Alcañiz on 23 May 1809, but the French commander was to turn the tide and defeat the Spaniard at Maria and Belchite the following month. Blake subsequently resigned his command of the Army of Catalonia after failing to come to the timely relief of the garrison at Gerona. In April 1810 he was given command of the Army of the Centre (at Cádiz); he was defeated at Baza that November but performed well at the Battle of Albuera in May 1811 and, as a result, was given command of the Army of Valencia. On assuming this new command, Blake immediately encountered hostility from the former Commander-in-Chief, the Marquis del Palacio. Palacio was a local man who questioned the suitability of Blake's nomination as an 'outsider'. Furthermore, he was convinced that the armies should undertake a forward defence, in Castellón, with a main defensive position astride the road at Saguntum.

Blake, conversely, viewed the problem in more national, strategic terms. He was well versed with the intentions of both Wellington and Castaños to secure the border forts of Badajoz and Ciudad Rodrigo and therefore realised the importance of retaining French attention on the east coast by way of a distraction. He was equally convinced that Suchet, against a backdrop of troop withdrawals to support Napoleon's Russian Campaign, would not commence his planned invasion of Valencia and that the French focus would remain concentrated on thwarting the main allied effort on the Portuguese-Spanish border. Wellington shared this view, but Napoleon and Suchet saw it quite differently; the latter recalling that Blake had *'accelerated the completion of the immense works which the Valencians were throwing up in defence of their capital, and availed himself of the uninterrupted intercourse by sea, to procure arms, provisions, money, and every kind of assistance of which he stood in need. Taking advantage of the spirit of the inhabitants, he exited them to resist the advance of the French, and called out all the male population, between the ages of fifteen and fifty, for militia duty'.*

Defence of Valencia was the antithesis of the policies proposed by the Marquis del Palacio. However, Blake decided to shield his first line of defence by establishing a strong outpost on the ancient, but recently renovated Fort of Saguntum at Murviedro, about thirty kilometres north of the Valencia. In addition he placed two outposts at Peñiscola and Oropesa. Nevertheless, his main defences were on the south bank of the Guadalaviar (the modern River Turia), which ran along the northern walls of the city of Valencia.

Captain General Joaquín BLAKE y JOYES (Real Academia de la Historia, Madrid)

As autumn approached, Suchet's tasks and responsibilities in Aragón and Catalonia continued to be both demanding and geographically dispersed. In addition to providing support to Macdonald (who was replaced in October by General Charles Decaen) in the north against a resurgent Army of Catalonia under General Luis Lacy, he also had to garrison Saragossa, Tortosa, Lérida and Tarragona. From the remaining available troops in his large Army, he handpicked 25,000 men for the Valencian offensive. He commenced his advance on 15 September and moved south on three routes; the main body concentrated at Tortosa and moved on the coast road with the field artillery; the second marched on the mountain route through Alcañiz and Morella and then linked up with the coast road at Castellón; and the final group went via Teruel, having departed from upper Aragón and Saragossa. The siege artillery remained at Tortosa until called forward in early October.

This last group, only 5,000 strong, were taking a fearful risk for had Blake come north in strength and challenged them the upshot would have been unavoidable. However, Blake's plan dictated otherwise and Suchet noted that they *'had no choice but to resort to the road from Tortosa which runs along the seashore, since the train could not proceed by any other; but the forts of Peñiscola and Oropesa presented two obstacles in the way: the former was, fortunately for us, at some distance from the road, and it was possible to mask it, and thereby to neutralise its influence. But the fort of Oropesa had full command of the road'.*

The Town and Castle at Oropesa (Suchet Memoirs)

Suchet tasked the commander of his Neapolitan Division, General Claude Antoine Compère, to capture the structure and clear the road for the French artillery and supply convoys, while he continued south with the balance of his force.   At Oropesa, in addition to the medieval Fort, there was a gun tower about a kilometre to the south-east; Compère blockaded the two defensive structures, cutting their communication. Major Michaud, the French engineer, detected a weak point in the Fort's defences; many of the houses lay close to the main gate and were not overlooked by any of the Fort's walls. With the French siege train still some days away, Compère decided to exploit this weakness and storm the fortress.   The commander of the Pompeii Battalion, with 130 grenadiers, thirty infantry armed with trenching tools, and a company of sappers entered the village and forced the Spanish defenders back to the Fort. Having loopholed the buildings near the main gate, the infantry tried to keep the heads of the defenders down long enough to enable the sappers to lay a charge and blow the gate. The attempt failed and many of the attackers were killed in the process.

Following this disappointment, Compère resigned himself to more traditional methods and work began almost immediately on the trenches and parallels in anticipation of the arrival of the heavy guns. Major Charrue, commanding Compère's artillery, provided some support with a few field guns but many French soldiers were killed by the sustained and accurate fire from the Fort's ramparts. By 9 October the works were complete and three 24-pounder guns, which had only arrived a few hours earlier, were moved into place.

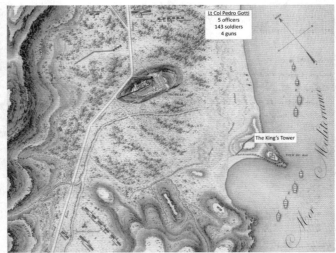

The Fort at Oropesa and the King's Tower – note the proximity of the Fort to the road.

Early on 10 October Suchet returned to Oropesa, with 500 Polish soldiers from the Legion of the Vistula, arriving just in time to witness the devastating effect of modern Napoleonic artillery against ancient walls. By midday the north wall had collapsed completely and Major Michalowski readied his Poles for the assault when, all of a sudden, the white flag appeared. Content the road was now open, Suchet returned to Saguntum with instructions to order the defenders of the King's Tower to surrender. Lieutenant Campillo, the commander in the tower, refused and Compère was left with no choice but to begin siege works to batter the young officer and his small garrison into submission. Before digging could commence however, *HMS Magnificent,* a 74-gun warship (commanded by Captain George Eyre) and a number of smaller Spanish vessels hove into view. Compère needed no time to appreciate how naval gunfire could support the Tower and its gallant defenders and elected to storm the place that night. The attack by the Poles failed completely and Compère, aware of the risks, decided to move some of the heavy guns onto unprotected platforms to batter the Tower. They were ready to open on 12 October but were soon countered by the accurate naval gunfire; however, the French guns had done enough to convince young Campillo to order the immediate abandonment of the Tower. His gallant Company were evacuated by small boats from the shore and rowed to the waiting vessels. Oropesa was in French hands and the siege train could now continue south to Saguntum.

The King's Tower. Built in 1542 by the great military engineer of the Valencian Renaissance, D. José Cervellón.

It was commanded by Lieutenant Campillo and manned by 60 grenadiers of the Savoya Regiment and 20 gunners.

Saguntum had been one of the most important towns in ancient and Moorish Spain but during the Middle Ages the city had declined and the Fort, which had held up Hannibal during the 2nd Punic Wars, was abandoned. Murviedro, a small town of 6,000 inhabitants was all that remained. Nevertheless, the citadel remained a naturally strong defensive position, protected by cliffs in many places. Enough remained of the Iberian and Moorish walls to be able to construct a series of new defences and the fortress, renamed San Fernando de Sagunto, had been completely rebuilt. A year's work had transformed the citadel into a tenable fortress, even if the design was asymmetrical, somewhat unscientific and by no means completed at the commencement of the siege. Colonel Luis Andriani was in command of the garrison which consisted of about 2,500 men, fourteen guns and three howitzers.

Saguntum Fort, Murviedro and the R. Palancia in the foreground (Suchet's Memoirs)

As early as 23 September Suchet's advance guard, led by General Isidore Harispe, had taken control of Murviedro, driving the isolated pockets of defenders back into the fortress. General Giuseppe Palombini's Italian Division covered the right flank and took control of Petrés (where Suchet established his headquarters) and Gilet, while Habert's Division crossed the river on the French left flank. Cavalry reconnaissance was sent further south and advanced to within ten kilometres of Valencia, meeting no resistance, for generals José Lardizábal and José San Juan (commanding the Spanish cavalry) had withdrawn in the face of the French advance to their respective positions on the River Guadalaviar.

Suchet decided to capture the Fort of Saguntum before moving south to engage Blake on the latter's chosen ground. The irregularity of the structure enticed him to attempt an assault without waiting for his siege artillery. With small arms and ladders the first attack was delivered during the night of 27-28 September; however, the main assaulting columns were discovered by a Spanish patrol some time before the prescribed hour of attack. Forced to initiate proceedings prematurely, the attackers had lost surprise and despite the distraction of the two diversionary attacks and the deployment of the French reserve, the assault was a complete failure.

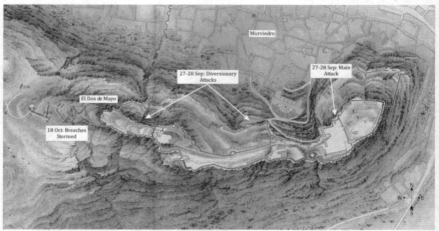

Saguntum Fort and the French attacks (Belmas)

Suchet accepted the inevitable and ordered the capture of Oropesa at any cost in order to open the way for the siege guns. However, the arrival of the heavy ordnance and stores was to take another two weeks, during which time Suchet's force was, to all intents and purposes, immobile. Blake now faced a dilemma; with the invading French Army at a standstill before him he was under mounting pressure to do something. He had two options: attack the force in an attempt to lift the siege or penetrate Aragón and cut off Suchet's lines of communication. Having tried and failed to get British naval support to land a small expeditionary force on the Levante coast and given the poor morale and operational effectiveness of elements of his force, namely the Murcians under General Mahy, Blake was more inclined to the latter option. Although his plans were, on the face of it, relatively timid they were designed to pose a serious threat to the French rear.

Suchet was, however, more concerned with Blake's attempts to threaten his camp at Saguntum and he despatched Palombini with his entire Division supported by Baron Robert's Brigade to counter Blake's moves in the direction of Segorbe and Benaguacil. This they achieved with relative ease. Suchet now turned his attention back to the Fort at Saguntum but he still had to wait another ten days for the siege guns. Valée and General Rogniat (the new Engineer Commander) arrived on 11 October, a day ahead of the train; they scrutinised the plans of their subordinates and concurred with the plan to attack the structure from the west but made several adjustments, in order to provide greater protection to the men digging, riveting and arming the battery positions. They also decided to use the steepness of the hill to their advantage by marking the battery positions well forward, shortening the distance to the walls and making it difficult for the defenders to use their guns against this work, as they would have to fire in negative elevation. Although the French made full use of this advantage, this in turn forced them to utilise a number of mortars and howitzers to overcome the problems presented by the significant elevation to the Fort's walls from their battery positions. On the night of 16 October a number of battery positions (1 to 4, Map 3) were ready and a total of ten guns, howitzers and mortars were moved into place.

Colonel Sanchez Cicernos, the second in command of the defence, recorded that *'On the 16th the enemy placed in the batteries, twelve pieces of 24, eight mortars and howitzers and this day they brought up the ammunition. The morning of the 17th at the break of dawn, the enemy greeted us with a terrible discharge of cannon, mortar and howitzer which was extensive and began to cause casualties to various individuals, I received the first, a strong bruise in the right leg from a stone that had already injured the artillery commander'*. The bombardment continued all day and despite quickly dislodging the repaired works, they made little impression on the old stone Moorish walls. Suchet noted that *'the breach was not much enlarged on the first day, though each of our cannon fired a hundred and fifty balls; we had to renew the fire the following day'*. Andriani moved seven infantry companies to the west of the Fort and they played a constant fire on the heads of the saps from the Dos de Mayo Battery and the Tower of San Pedro. As the assault trenches came closer to the walls and effective musket range, the French began to suffer appreciable casualties.

The fire continued until late into the afternoon on the 18 October; Valée and Rogniat reconnoitred the resulting breach and reported to Suchet that it was practicable. The French commander ordered an assault for five that evening. It was a brave call, for the breach was still very narrow and the debris, in large stones and sections, would hinder rather than help the assaulting infantry. One hundred hand-picked-men from the 5e Léger, the 114e and 117e Ligne collected in the late afternoon under Colonel Mathis, and a reserve, of four hundred men from the Italian Division, were placed under Major Olini. The Spanish, suspecting an assault, began to retrench the ramparts with sandbags, answering every French shot with a volley of musket fire and taunting their besiegers to *'come to close quarters with them'*. Rogniat recalled, that *'the enemy were presented on the summit with a lot of resolution, neither our rifle bullets nor our canon could dislodge them or impede them in their incessant reestablishment of the walls with sandbags...'*

The assault went in on schedule but was quickly bogged down; the many officers leading the assaulting parties left the cover of the trenches to cross the remaining 70 meters up to the base of the wall and breach. They were quickly overwhelmed by the weight of the defenders' fire and, as they could only advance two-men abreast, they could not mass sufficient numbers at the base. The few that arrived could find no solid footing. Once the initial momentum was spent, Habert wasted no time in concluding that the attack would not succeed. He ordered the assaulting parties back to the trenches and Suchet pondered his next move. He could not afford to squander soldiers from his minimal invasion force and the two failed attempts had done little for French morale. Suchet was clear that there would not be another assault until the curtain, in front of the Dos de Mayo Battery, had been indisputably breached. That would inevitably take time.

This delay in siege operations unexpectedly played into French hands, for Blake was under increasing pressure from the Valencians to relieve the garrison at Saguntum and undertake some form of pre-emptive strike against Suchet's forces. At the same time news arrived that Wellington had been forced to postpone the major allied offensive in the west, leaving the French free to move formations in support operations on the East Coast. Blake, fearing that Suchet's forces were poised to receive considerable reinforcement, decided to act. He penned plans for the divisions of General José Obispo and General Nicolás Mahy to link up and act as an advance guard. They were to move down the Segorbe road, in order to attack the French rear while Blake, with the balance of his Army, moved to attack simultaneously from the south. As the formations were manoeuvring to commence the advance, Blake received new intelligence which alerted the situation. His operations in upper Aragón were bearing fruit with significant victories by José Duran and Juan Martin Diez (El Empecinado) at Calatayud and Almunia and by Francisco Espoz y Mina on General Philippe Severoli's Division at Ayerbe. Espoz's Navarrese Division was now threatening to capture Teruel; an unacceptable state of affairs which ultimately forced Suchet's hand.

Palombini's first brigade, along with his divisional artillery, Robert's Brigade and General André Boussart's Cuirassiers were sent north to avert disaster. News of this movement prompted Blake to change his original plans; Obispo was now instructed to move via Sancti-Espiritu, by way of a diversion, and the Army of Valencia was then to execute a general advance upon the vastly smaller French force south of Saguntum, in the Val de Jesús. It was a reasonable plan and may have succeeded had Palombini not suddenly re-appeared the night prior to the Valencian attack. Both Suchet and Blake were unaware of General Louis Musnier's (commanding the garrison at Saragossa) bold move to send Mazzucheli, with a brigade sized force to Teruel in order to provide relief to the beleaguered French forces and secure the town. Palombini was thus able to retrace his steps and provide Suchet, on the eve of the battle, the opportunity to strengthen his main force and to despatch an additional brigade (that of Robert) to support Baron Gregorz Jozef Chlopicki's Brigade at Sancti-Espiritu. This latter action was to have significant consequences the following day.

Blake's and Suchet's Orders of Battle for 25 October 1811

BLAKE - 28,044 (Source: Arcón)

Left Wing

C. O'Donnell — Luengo *2 x 8 pdr guns and 2 x 7 inch howitzers*

Villacampa *[2ᵈ Princesa(2), 2ᵈ Soria(2)]*

San Juan *[Cazadores a caballo de Valencia(1 sqn), Dragones del Rey(3 sqns), Voluntarios de Molina(1) Real Cuerpo de Zapadores (1 coy), 2 x 4 pdr guns.]*

Miranda

Gervasio Gasca *Linea, Cazadores a Caballo de Valencia (1 sqn), Real Cuerpo de Zapadores (1 coy), 2 x 4 pdr guns.]*

Miranda *[2ᵈ Cazadores de Valencia(1), 1ˢᵗ & 2ᵈ Infantry de Valencia, 1ˢᵗ & 2ᵈ Voluntarios de Castilla.]*

Rearguard - Infantry de Avila(1).

O'Ronan *[2ᵈ Voluntarios de Aragón(1), Cazadores de Valencia(1), Dragones del Rey (1 sqn).]*

Obispo *[Tiradores de Doyle(1), Cazadores Campo de Cariñena(2), 2ᵈ Avila(1), 1ˢᵗ Aragón(1), Voluntarios de Daroca(1), Dragones de la Reina(1 sqn), Husares de Aragón(2 sqns).]*

Left Wing - Reserve

Mahy — Ibarra *2 x 4 pdr, 2 x 8 pdr and 2 x 7 inch howitzers*

Santiago Terreros *[Tiradores de Cádiz(1), Voluntarios de Burgos(1), Dragones de Madrid(1 sqn).]*

Conde de Montijo *[1ˢᵗ Badajoz(2), Cuenca(2), Real Cuerpo de Zapadores.]*

Creagh de Lacy *[La Corona(1), Alcazar de San Juan(1), Real Cuerpo de Zapadores(1 coy), Dragones de la Reina(1 sqn).]*

Osorio *[Dragones de Pavia(2 sqns), Dragones de Granada(2 sqns), Hussares de Fernando VII(1 sqn).]*

Right Wing

Lardizabal — *[2 x 4pdr, 2 x 8pdr and 2 x 7 inch howitzers.]*

Lardizabal *[Murcia(2), Badajoz(2), 1 x 4 pdr and 1 x 8pdr guns.]*

Prieto *[Africa(2), Tiradores de Cuenca(1).]*

Vanguard - Saravia: Ligero de Campomayor(1).

Zayas — Gómez *[2 x 4pdr, 2 x 8 pdr and 2 x 7 inch howitzers.]*

Zayas *[2ᵈ Reales Guardias Españoles(1), 4ᵗʰ Reales Guardias Españoles(1).]*

Polo *[Voluntarios de Cuidad Rodrigo(1), 1ˢᵗ and 2ᵈ Patria(2), Imperial de Toledo(1).]*

De Hautregard *[1ˢᵗ Reales Guardias Walonas(1), 1ˢᵗ Legion Estranjera(1), Real Cuerpo de Zapadores(1 coy).]*

Vanguard - Favré d' Aunoy: Cazadores Reunidos.

Loy *[Granaderos a caballo(2 sqns), Caballeria del Rey(1 sqn), Husares de Casilla(1 sqn), 3ᵉ escuadron de artilleria de caballo, 1 x 4pdr and 1 7 inch howitzer.]*

Chacón *[Dragones de Numancia(4 sqns), Provisional de Caballeria(3 sqns), Caballeria de Alcántara(1 sqn), Husares Españoles(1 sqn), Husares de Granada(1 sqn).]*

Del Río *[Caballeria de Cuenca(3 sqns), Cazadores a caballo de Montaña(1 sqn).]*

Right Wing - Reserve

Caro

Velasco *[3ˢᵗ Voluntarios de Castilla(1), 3ˢᵗ Avila(1), Provisional Infanteria de linea(7 coys), Real Cuerpo de Zapadores (1 coy), artilleria compania 2 x 4pdr, 1 x 8 pdr and 1 x 7 inch howitzer.]*

Liory *[3ˢᵗ Infante Don Carlos, Provisional Infanteria de ligera(6 coys), artilleria seccion 2 x 8pdr.]*

SUCHET - 18,333 (Source: Arcón)

Left Wing - Vall de Jesús - 9,468

3 Harispe — Duchand *[5e Artilleria de cheval 6 x 4 pdr.]*

Paris *[7e Ligne(3), 116e Ligne(3), 3e Legion de Vistula(2).]*

Cristophe *[4e Hussars(3 sqns)].*

4 Habert — Delaporte *[3e Artilleria a pied 6 x 8pdr.]*

Montmarie *[5e Léger(2), 16e Ligne(3), 117 e Ligne(1).]*

Cristophe *[24e Dragoons(2 sqns)].*

IT Palombini

IT Barbieri - Note 2 *[2e (IT) Léger(2), 4e (IT) Ligne(2).]*

(-) Boussart *[13e Cuirassiers(3 sqns).]*

Right Wing - Sancti Espiritu - 3,579 *[2e Vistula - Note 3]*

Chlopicki *[44e Ligne(2), 114e Ligne(1), Dragoons de Napoleon(3 sqns).]*

Robert *[114e Ligne(1), 1ˢᵗ Vistula(1), Elite Battalion (1).]*

Reserve Forces in Gilet - 2,343

NP Compère *[1ˢᵗ IT Artilleria Ligera a Caballo - 6 guns.]*

NP Ferrier *[1e (NP) Ligne del Rey(1), 1e (NP) Ligne del Reina(1), 1e (NP) Léger (1).]*

Millet *[121e Ligne(1), 13e Cuirassiers(1coy).]*

Fondzielski *[1e Vistula(1), Fusiliers (1).]*

[1ˢᵗ and 2ᵈ Cazadores a Caballo(2 sqns).]

Forces Maintaining Cordon at Saguntum Fort - 4,419

Bronikowski *[2/117e Ligne, 3/117e Ligne, 16e Ligne (3 companies) 2e Vistula (5 companies)* Note 1*]*

Balathier *[Italian 1/5e, 2/5e, 1/6e & 2/6e* Note 2* Ligne.]*

Valée *[Artillery of 1st & 4th Divisions and Reserve.]*

Rogniat *[6 engineer companies]*

Notes:
1. The 2nd brigade of Habert's Division.
2. The 2nd brigade of Palombini's Division.
3. Voltigeur companies of 2e Vistula came down from Almenara to act as hinge between Chlopicki and Robert.

At two in the afternoon on 24 October a three-cannon salvo was fired from the walls of the city of Valencia; this acted as the signal for the Spanish forces to advance to their initial positions. Blake left his headquarters and took the

Camino Real to El Puig, where he established his new headquarters in the Castle on his arrival at 10 p.m. A makeshift hospital was set up in Rafelbuñol and preparations were made for a number of carts to transport the wounded to hospitals in Valencia and Bétera. By nightfall all the Spanish forces were in place except Obispo who was still heading south from his original mission. *HMS Minstrel*, an 18-gun corvette, and six Spanish gunboats supported Blake's force along the Playa del Puig coastline. Suchet did not hesitate to take up the offer of battle; he left General Nicolas Bronikowski in command to maintain the siege at Saguntum and moved, with the balance of his force, to the north end of the Val de Jesús.

During the night Blake had been apprised of Obispo's failure to appear on the Spanish left wing and had given orders for Edmundo O'Ronan's Brigade to deploy in his stead. At 6.30 a.m. on 25 October, Blake came down from the Castillo at El Puig and went to the Cartuja de Ara Christi Monastery where he delivered the final orders for the advance. This was to commence on the left with San Juan's all-arms vanguard at 7.30 a.m. followed by the main body of the left wing thirty minutes later. General Pedro Villacampa was to advance using the Camino Liria as his axis with General José Miranda to his right. These two divisions were under the overall command of General Carlos O'Donnell. The Spanish right wing, which had less distance to travel, was allocated start times of 8.30 a.m. for Lardizabal's Division and 9 a.m. for General José Zayas's Division. Caro's cavalry preceded Lardizabal by about twenty minutes, using the Camino Real as its axis. Lardizabal was to take his reinforced battery forward and establish a new battery position from which to engage the French main body. In view of Obispo's failure to show, O'Ronan was ordered to move at around 9 a.m. and probe the defile of Sancti-Espiritu, while General Juan Creagh de Lacy's Division (from Mahy's reserve) was tasked to replace them on the Cabezbort feature.

The screen of French tirailleurs and a squadron of the 4e Hussars were already engaged in bickering fire for about two hours with the Spanish skirmishers and elements of Caro's and Lardizabal's vanguard (6 to 8 a.m.). However, Suchet remained confused as to Spanish intentions and, at about 8 a.m. he decided to move south, up the Camino Real, to a position just short of the first line of inns at 'Hostalets' to try and get a better feel for the Spanish dispositions. The area was covered with a combination of olive and carob trees, and visibility on the flat plains was limited but the small hillock of 'El Hostalet', between the Camino Liria and the hills of the Montenegro, was in plain sight. Suchet arrived in time to witness San Juan's advance guard retaking the hillock after evicting the cavalry Suchet had personally posted. Suchet quickly appreciated the tactical value of any rise, however modest, on the featureless plains and immediately ordered Harispe to retake the mound. It was about 9 a.m.

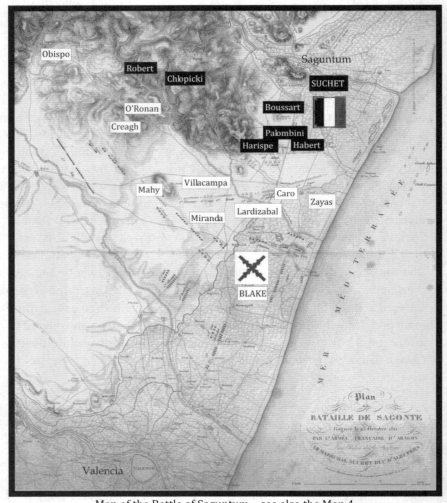

Map of the Battle of Saguntum – see also the Map 4
This is Suchet's map which depicts the forces at numerous stages of the Battle. The overlay depicts the approximate areas for the various formations at about 10 a.m.

Since occupying the feature, Villacampa had deployed additional skirmishers to screen those of the French who were coming down the slopes of the Montenegro hills to his left. San Juan had also deployed additional skirmishers to the front and two companies of Molina and one of sappers on the hill itself; while the Dragones del Rey were on the left and two 4-pounder guns to the right. The balance of the Molina Regiment was behind the hill in reserve. (It was these forces that Harispe engaged so hotly at around 9 a.m. when he was first ordered to capture the 'El Hostalet', not those of Lardizabal as traditionally reported). Critically however, Miranda was having considerable difficulty negotiating the terrain, which contained several ditches and walls, and his soldiers were unable to advance at the same pace as the divisions of Villacampa to his left and Lardizabal to his right. This caused a large gap to open between the three divisions and a corresponding loss of mutual support (See Map 4).

On the Spanish left, O'Ronan began to move up the defile between the El Caballo and Coll de la Calderona and was suddenly surprised by the 44e Ligne drawn-up across the road ready to receive the advancing Spaniards. The regiment had in fact been positioned covering the defile since September. It was about 9.30 a.m. and, after a short exchange of fire followed by the arrival of the balance of Chlopicki's Brigade, O'Ronan elected to withdraw back the way he had come. Chlopicki sent Robert after him and took his brigade, plus the three squadrons of Dragoons de Napoleon, and headed south further down the track to a better vantage point from where he could survey the plains below. While this small but intense action had been taking place, both Zayas and Lardizabal (on the Spanish right) had advanced to the areas of Puzol and Hostalets respectively. Suchet, once he had given orders to Harispe to take the 'El Hostalet', had withdrawn back north up the Camino Real. He was conscious that Zayas was trying, with the aid of the naval gunfire, to get around the French left flank and approach the town of Murviedro. With the noticeable gap created by Miranda's troubled advance in the centre, he resolved to split the Spanish left and right with Palombini's Division, which was now called forward.

Back on the French right, Chlopicki arrived at his vantage point and witnessed the battle for the of the 'El Hostalet' hillock, which the 7e Ligne had just recaptured. O'Donnell reacted by sending Villacampa's four battalions and four additional guns forward, while the Dragones del Rey advanced to prevent elements of the 116e Ligne from supporting the 7e Ligne on the feature itself.

Colonel Lanzarote, commanding the Dragones del Rey, stated in his report that *'the ground was completely unsuitable for cavalry and the 116e repulsed the Spanish dragoons with ease'*. Lanzarote, while trying to rally and regroup for a second attempt, was suddenly and unexpectedly charged by the 4e Hussars and then peppered by canister. The dragoons fled and this seemingly insignificant episode ignited the series of events that led to the collapse of the Spanish left and ultimately the loss of the battle. With San Juan's Dragones in a desperate situation, the Hussars began to pursue the fleeing cavalry and O'Donnell, considering his entire wing in jeopardy, ordered a retreat upon Mahy's advance guard, provided by General Santiago Terreros's Brigade, at the Barranco del Pixador.

Baron Gregorz Jozef CHLOPICKI   Major General André BOUSSART

The French Hussars made better speed than the infantry, but soon realised that Villacampa's men had rallied behind Mahy's vanguard and that General Casimiro Loy's cavalry had taken the bold decision to charge and were heading back toward the 'El Hostalet' with the intention of capturing the feature. Harispe ordered Chef d'Esquadron Duchand, commanding the horse artillery, to deploy forward and once again engage at close quarters with canister and grape. They had some initial success but were too far advanced and, when the 4e Hussars charge was driven back by the mass of almost a thousand cavalry, they lost three of their guns to the advancing Spanish. It was about 11 a.m. and at this moment the battle hung in the balance. Harispe's infantry, intimately supported by Palombini's Italians, held their nerve and their ground; the latter defeating the cavalry charge with well-sustained fire. Suchet had returned to this part of the field to witness the Spanish recovery and rallied Boussart's cuirassiers. Once released, the cuirassiers thundered into the Spanish and their commander, Colonel De Gonneville recalled, *'At first I feared that my men would be discouraged by the rout of the 4e Hussars and our first squadron; but I was speedily reassured, and experienced the most intoxicating sensation that it is possible to feel on the field of battle'*. The rapid follow-up by Harispe's infantry and hussars recovered the three lost guns and continued all the way to the banks of the Picador stream during which they captured five Spanish guns and three standards. Caro was wounded and taken prisoner and O'Donnell's left wing was unhinged. The initiative had firmly swung back in favour of the French.

Events on the Spanish far left were also about to have a significant impact. Obispo had finally emerged from the village of Naquera, just in time to see O'Ronan's force withdrawing at speed in the face of Robert's Brigade, which had emerged from the defile of Sancti-Espiritu. Obispo deployed and brought Robert's advance to an abrupt halt. Outnumbered by more than two to one, Robert began to fall back; bayoneting a small number of Spanish prisoners who tried to take advantage of the situation and make good their escape. Meanwhile, at the Pixador ravine, about half of O'Donnell and Miranda's forces had rallied behind Mahy's advance guard and halted Harispe's vigorous advance, providing the opportunity for Caro's cavalry to overrun Harispe's left flank and take his artillery. However, these two brief advantages were soon undone by Mahy who, initially fearing that Robert would outflank the feature as he pursued O'Ronan, had ordered Creagh to abandon the Cabezbort. It was a monumental error which opened the door for Chlopicki who, until this point, had been content to watch O'Donnell and Mahy but he was keen (despite orders to the contrary) for some of the action.

Chlopicki states in his report that at about noon he advanced upon an impressive array of Spanish troops deployed at the foot of Los Germanells and was intent on attacking them. (This contradicts Oman, who accorded considerable praise to Chlopicki's early attacks on O'Donnell's flank as a significant contributory factor in the subsequent collapse and rout of the Spanish left wing). Much to his surprise the Spanish did not wait for him; Mahy quickly abandoned the feature, and with it, any hope of holding the Spanish left.

O'Ronan, Obispo and Creagh made good their escape into the mountains to the west. Robert's force was spent but it took a considerable time (nearly two hours) for Harispe to combine forces with Chlopicki and chase the already routed forces of O'Donnell that had fled behind Mahy's reserve. In fact, Suchet had held them back because events on the French left were far from settled. However, once released, Harispe's and Chlopicki's formations, supported by about one hundred French hussars and dragoons, renewed the advance taking nearly 2,000 Spanish prisoners (mainly Mahy's troops) and continuing for some kilometres until they were finally stopped by skirmishers of the regiment of Cuenca and Voluntarios de Molina who deployed across the Bétera road. It was about 4.30 p.m.

View north from the walls of the Cartuja Monastery, from where the Walloon Guards covered the withdrawal of the Spanish left wing

Blake was watching the battle from the heights at El Puig and could clearly see his left wing in full flight and accordingly issued orders for the right wing to withdraw. Brigadier General Montmarie finally took possession of Puzol after a fierce fight during which the Spanish yielded 800 prisoners. Zayas's Division had to withdraw in contact and was assisted in this by the Walloon Guards and the Foreign Legion (Legión Extranjero) and one 8-pounder gun sited by Zayas as a reserve some distance behind the village of Puzol. Lardizabal's left flank was now dangerously exposed by the collapse of the Spanish left wing, and he began an orderly withdrawal in the face of ruthless harassment by the 24e

Dragoons which, fortuitously for the Spanish, were constrained by the dense vegetation and irrigation ditches on either side of the Camino Real. Lardizabal redeployed at the Cartuja, with General José Liori's Brigade, and together they thwarted further French advances. Meanwhile Zayas had gone firm at El Puig with General Manuel Velasco. However, there was to be no rearguard action; Blake, capitalising on the two-hour lull in the fighting, had redeployed Zayas with Velasco at El Puig, and despatched an aide-de-camp to Mahy instructing him to do the same at Germanells with the Murcians and the remains of the Valencian Army. Lardizabal, who had taken a safer position back at Puebla de Farnals, moved forward and engaged Palombini in order to distract Suchet's attention from Mahy at Germanells. In this Blake was completely successful. Suchet reacted by despatching Harispe to envelope Lardizábal and Zayas and cut their retreat to Valencia but Blake, acutely aware of the danger of an exposed left flank, had already ordered a general retreat to Valencia.

Saguntum Castle from the roof of Suchet's Headquarters at Petres (Castell dells Agulló)

The next morning Suchet returned to Saguntum Fort and sent a summons to Andriani and, after a short discussion about terms, the garrison surrendered. The morale of the defenders had been severely shaken by the failure of their countrymen the day prior and by the effect that the French siege artillery was now having on the makeshift walls. Following the loss of both the battle and Fort of Saguntum, Blake still had 22,000 men under arms but their morale was understandably dubious. To Suchet, an immediate attempt on Valencia was a tempting proposition but when he had counted up his losses, deducted men to garrison Saguntum and detached a brigade to escort the prisoners to Tortosa, he was left with only 15,000 combatants. He was reluctant, even at this stage, to call up Ficatier's Brigade from Segorbe and Oropesa as he was determined to keep open his lines of communication. He decided instead to consolidate his gains and summoned both General Philippe Severoli's and General Charles Reille's divisions from Aragón in anticipation of the next phase of his offensive. However he required Napoleonic approval before he could summon and move them and this was to take time. This delay allowed Blake to take stock of his position and to strengthen the defensive lines in and around Valencia in anticipation of the inevitable follow-up attack by Suchet's triumphant forces.

History has recorded Blake's performance harshly. Oman records that Blake sent 6,000 to 7,000 men to Aragón "to paralyse the movements of more than 20,000 French". Then he adds that the operation "never prevented him [Suchet] from executing any operation of primary importance". This misses the point that the capture of Valencia *was* the primary goal and that Suchet could not attempt this until he was reinforced by the divisions of Severoli and Reille, the very forces the mission to Aragón had engaged and made unavailable. The two French divisions arrived in late December, delaying the campaign by a full two months. Throughout this time Napoleon had been pressurising Joseph to provide tangible support to Suchet; Soult, characteristically, swerved the issue of providing forces, while Joseph's command was already stretched to the limit in and around Madrid, so the burden fell to Marshal Auguste Marmont, commanding the Army of Portugal. His redirection of three key divisions (Montbrun, Foy and Sarrut) to support D'Armagnac's Division (from the Army of the Centre) was to open the window of opportunity for Wellington and enable him, in January 1812, to pounce and capture Ciudad Rodrigo, the northern key to Spain.

This version of the Battle of Saguntum differs from the hitherto accepted accounts of the battle. It is based on extensive research by José Luis Arcón Dominguez, during which he has unquestioningly confirmed, that Blake's objectives were entirely to the south and east of Montenegro and not through the mountains of Calderona. Although there is evidence that it had been Blake's original intention of turning the French right, he changed his plans at some stage prior to the 24th October 1811. Oman admits that, 'There are terrible difficulties as to the timing of the Battle of Saguntum' (vol. V. p. 36, note 1). Oman interprets Arteche and uses Suchet and Schepeler as his principal sources but not the battle reports of O'Donnell, Miranda, San Juan, Obispo and Lardizabal as well as three other official Spanish diaries all of which (unanimously) confirm that Blake's objectives were confined to the valley floor between the Montenegro and the Mediterranean Sea.

The divisions of Severoli and Reille arrived in the region on 24 December increasing Suchet's force to 33,000 men; about 10,000 more than the remnants of Blake's combined armies. On Christmas Day, all Suchet's divisions advanced south towards the Spanish lines and the city of Valencia. His plan of attack was ambitious; he would force his passage at two points across the River Guadalaviar and trap Blake's entire army. In essence it was encirclement, with one column forcing the crossing to the east between Valencia and the sea and a second to the west. Both columns would then join up, south of the city, completing the closure.

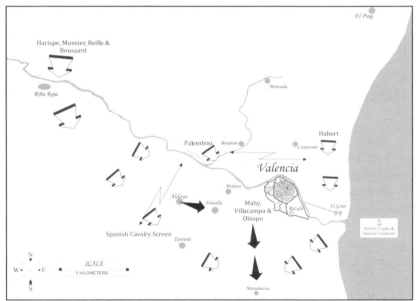

The French encirclement of Blake's Forces and the City of Valencia ~ December 1812

By first light on 26 December French engineers had constructed both light and heavy bridges across the Guadalaviar at Riba Roja and half the French force, consisting of the divisions of Harispe, Musnier, Reille and all the French cavalry, had crossed. Blake's vedettes had been driven-in early during the operation, depriving him of intelligence on French intentions and strengths. As the day unfolded, it became clear that elements of this right flanking force

(Harispe) were moving rapidly south to Torrent to cut off the road to Alicante, and one brigade from Musnier's Division and the cavalry were preparing to follow. The second of Musnier's brigades, that of Robert, was holding the bridge waiting for Reille's Division to cross. This intelligence was fairly conclusive but Blake failed to act upon it, being entirely preoccupied with events on the Spanish right, where Habert's column had already crossed the estuary of the Guadalaviar and was beginning to swing west. Blake considered Habert the real danger and by the time he realised his mistake, the French main force was poised to join Habert and close the ring.

Valencia from the north bank of the River Guadalaviar

Elements of Blake's defending force realised French intentions slightly earlier than their commander. The Spanish divisions of Villacampa and Obispo recognized that they were about to be surrounded and abandoned their positions, racing south to escape the trap. About half of this Spanish force managed to break-out but the others were cut off. Meanwhile, Palombini was attempting to penetrate the Spanish lines at Mislata. His first attack stalled, but the Italian rallied his men and delivered a second, more determined assault, against Zayas whose division had been left exposed by the departure of Villacampa and Obispo. Blake tried to readjust his defence and recover the situation but, before long, realised it was hopeless and was compelled to recall both Zayas and Lardizabal back to the confines of Valencia.

Blake was now trapped and surrounded; he had 17,000 men (the divisions of Miranda, Zayas, Lardizabal and what was left of the reserve battalions) but his defensive task was extensive and Valencia's walls were not designed to withstand the rigours of a modern siege. By 1 January most of the French siege guns had arrived from Saguntum and Suchet opened trenches against the Fort of Monte Olivete and the southern point of the suburb of San Vincente. By 4 January seven batteries (1 to 7) had been established but Blake did not wait for these guns to open on the inadequate outer defences; instead he withdrew his entire force into the narrow confines of the city itself.

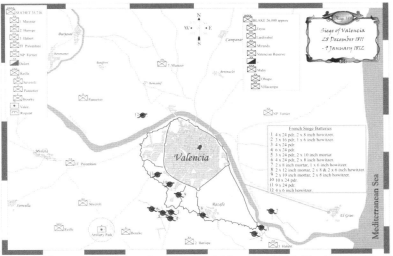

The Siege of Valencia ~28th December 1811 to 9th January 1812 (Peninsular War Atlas)

Suchet lost no time building fresh batteries (8 to 12) in the newly captured ground and, on 6 January, while the heavy guns battered the walls, the three mortar batteries fired over 1,000 shells into the city. Large numbers of civilians were killed or wounded. Suchet then sent a group to invite Blake to capitulate; he refused and the relentless bombardment continued for another two days. It was unethical but it was enough to convince the Spanish commander of the futility of further defiance and, on 9 January, the citadel and the city were handed over to the French. Blake himself was escorted straight to France and did not remain to take part in the formal surrender. Over 16,000 regular troops were made prisoner and transported north across the Pyrenees, marching in two columns under the escort of Pannetier's Brigade. No less than 374 cannon (mainly heavy guns from the city itself) and 21 colours were taken. It had taken Suchet only fourteen days to capture this vital city; his methods remain open to question but he was a man in a hurry. The French marshal had every reason to be satisfied but, in early January, he would have been unaware that the delay in capturing this first objective was to have far reaching strategic consequences.

The rapid capitulation of Valencia did, to an extent, save its inhabitants from the repugnant horrors of post siege licentiousness. With Valencia in French hands, Suchet informed Joseph that the services of the four divisions and artillery from the armies of the Centre and Portugal were no longer required. Suchet considered his Army, reinforced with the two strong divisions of Reille and Severoli, strong enough to tackle the Spanish 3rd Army (formerly the Army of Murcia) numbering slightly more than 6,000 men which was concentrating around Alicante. The Murcian Army consisted, in the main, of Mahy's corps-sized force, which had escaped the encirclement at Valencia.

Inexplicably, General Louis Montbrun chose to ignore his orders to return west and rejoin the Army of Portugal. In a display of personal ambition, he marched on Alicante; driving back General Manuel Freire from Elche. On 15 January, he came up against the town's fortifications which had been much improved in the preceding years. Inside the two forts were the divisions of Creagh, Obispo, Roche and Bassecourt, 6,000 regular and well armed troops. Outnumbered and lacking siege artillery, Montbrun quickly realised the futility of trying to capture the town and the palpable danger of outstaying his welcome and he withdrew, taking out his frustration on the local towns and villages as he went. This pointless foray delayed the return of this formation to the Tagus, denied Marmont a vital element of his force at a critical time and understandably incensed Suchet.

Having released Marmont's and Joseph's supporting divisions, Suchet set about planning the capture of Alicante unaware that two entirely unconnected events were to thwart his final conquest. The first was Napoleon's plans for his war with Russia and second was Wellington's early success in the Salamanca Campaign. Marshal Alexandre Berthier's directive of 14 January withdrew the whole of the Infantry of the Guard and all the Polish regiments in Spain and left large gaps in the armies of Soult, General Jean Dorsenne (North) and Suchet. For the latter, the loss of the six Polish battalions was a blow. An even greater disappointment, leaving a mere 9,000 men at his disposal, was the need to reunite Reille with Caffarelli to create a new Army of the Ebro and to redeploy Palombini to deal with the growing insurrection in southern Aragón.

Nevertheless, Suchet deployed Harispe (supported by Jacque Delort's Brigade) to Xativa with orders to watch the Spanish 3rd Army north of Alicante, but with the clear qualification not to advance too far south as there were many reports of yellow fever in the province of Murcia. Indeed, the contagion had reached Alicante and as far north as Alcoy by October 1811. Habert was sent to Gandia, from where he moved south and captured the small port and strong castle at Denia securing, due to Mahy's carelessness, 66 garrison artillery guns and 40 useful small boats in the process. He was instructed to remain in touch with Harispe, and support him if necessary. Habert established a garrison within the Castle and fitted out some of the boats as privateers. He would have been unaware, as he set about his work, that this was to be the most southerly French garrison Suchet's Army was to establish in the East Coast Campaign.

Denia Castle and Harbour ~ circa 1900

Musnier was directed north, initially to Peñiscola, but subsequently to maintain communications with the garrison at Tortosa. The job of probing Peñiscola (which remained in Spanish hands) therefore fell to Severoli and his force, consisting of five battalions and part of the large siege train from

Saguntum. Peñiscola, a cross between Mont Saint-Michel and Gibraltar, supported a Spanish garrison of over 1,000 men, mostly veterans. However, they were commanded by General Garcia Navarro, a man who had lost hope following the fall of Valencia. Severoli distributed his force along the coast and on the hills overlooking the fortress and, following Suchet's tactics from Valencia, decided to bombard the place and then issue a summons in the hope of an early success. The first battery of 12 heavy mortars was prepared and, on 28 January, it began a slow and relatively ineffectual fire upon the fortifications. On the night of 31 January, Lieutenant Colonel Plagniol began work on a long parallel, which ran north to south and culminated on the beach area in front of the isthmus. Work was rapid as the soil was sandy and the structure was made entirely of fascines and gabions; the gunners were quick to establish two batteries inside and another two on the heights.

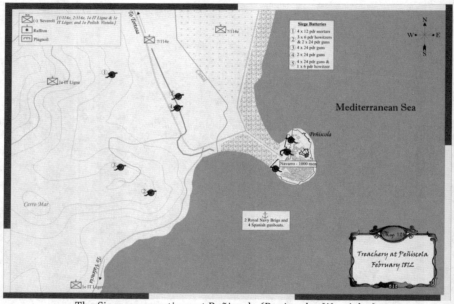

The Siege preparations at Peñiscola (Peninsular War Atlas)

The Royal Navy continued to re-supply the garrison and provide advice to Navarro who, in turn, expressed his concerns to Freire and Mahy in a series of letters. One such communiqué was captured by the French, in a small boat off the coast at Denia; the contents revealed Navarro's state of mind. Suchet, once apprised of the situation, immediately ordered Severoli to despatch a forceful summons to the garrison. This was received by Navarro on 2 February and he accepted the terms without delay. Expressing, rather lamely, that he wished to see Spain *'united under the protecting authority capable of terminating and repairing her calamities'*.

The fortified island of Peñiscola

The following day, the island was in French hands. Navarro's capitulation was nothing short of betrayal, providing a cheap and rapid accession for Suchet's depleted forces and enabling Severoli to be swiftly re-tasked. Suchet, still suffering from a badly healed wound from the Battle of Saguntum, fell ill before this new offensive could begin and by the end of April when he emerged from his sick bed, the situation in the Peninsula had swung back in favour of the allies. Suchet's immediate concern, following his return to health, was one of an administrative rather than a military nature. Napoleon had ordered Suchet to extract 200 million *reals* in war contributions from the Kingdom of Valencia. It was tedious task, which took up considerable amounts of the Army Commander's time in organisational and clerical work. Suchet was also embroiled in a constant struggle with Madrid to avoid having to provide additional forces from his Army to stem the tide of allied success in the west. He was quick to point out his special relationship with Paris and the fact that large numbers of reinforcements could only be realistically obtained from Soult's Army of the South.

In the meantime, Joseph O'Donnell (not to be confused with his brothers, Carlos O'Donnell who commanded a division at Sagunto and Valencia, or Henry O'Donnell who was undoubtedly the most capable of the three siblings) had been given command of the combined armies of Murcia and Valencia. He took advantage of the lull in hostilities to raise and train a force of about 20,000 men. Freire, now O'Donnell's second in command, had executed a series of raids; firstly on Baza in April and then, aided by the Royal Navy, on the south coast villages and ports as far west as Almunecar. Soult did nothing to prevent these raids as he was completely preoccupied with the idea that Wellington was about to invade Andalusia and had concentrated his forces and focus to the north and west.

Suchet having successfully fought off Joseph's demands to redistribute large numbers of his forces west in support of the Army of the Centre, still lacked sufficient strength to prosecute operations south of the line currently held by Harispe (Alcoy) and Habert (Denia). With a British expeditionary force rumoured to be approaching, any attempt to take the initiative was likely to end in disaster. This force was the long awaited Anglo-Sicilian diversion to the opening phase of the Salamanca Campaign; delayed by Lord Bentinck's hesitation, its arrival was, by mid July, imminent. Wellington had ordered O'Donnell to provide Roche's Division in support of this force and warned him to content himself with containing Suchet's force to his front and not to try anything that might upset the *status quo* within the region. However, O'Donnell had also been tasked to maintain contact with Suchet and in early July he considered the opportunity to his front simply too good to pass up. Faced with a number of possible disembarkation sites for the Anglo-Sicilian expeditionary force, Suchet had been compelled to retain a reaction force north of Valencia that could counter, either in support of Decaen or within his own area of operations, as required. In consequence, the balance of his force was spread thinly across the frontage and this tempted O'Donnell to make productive use of Roche's Division, which had returned to Alicante, in advance of the balance of the Anglo-Sicilian Force and was, once again, placed under O'Donnell's command.

O'Donnell's plan was ambitious; he intended to surround the forward elements of Harispe's Division, at Ibi and Castalla, and destroy them before the reserve could be deployed from Alcoy. From his hideout in the northern hills, General Luis Bassecourt was to close on Biar and Ibi and distract the reserve at the vital moment. By way of a further distraction, all available sea transports were to deploy to Denia, Gandia and as far north as Cullera to create a diversion and keep Habert's and Suchet's reserve occupied. The Spanish approached on three routes, marching through the night of 20 July; O'Donnell's group, consisting of three brigade-sized formations arrived in front of the French early the following morning, exhausted from their efforts and unaware of the whereabouts of Santisteban's column.

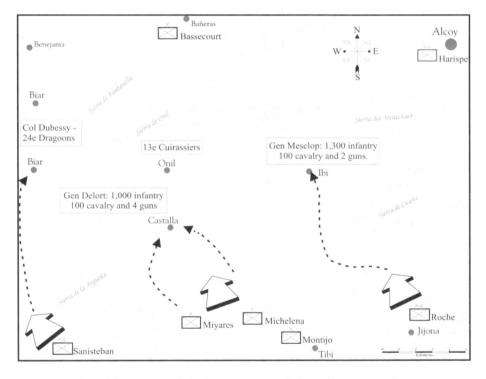

As the Spanish appeared, Delort evacuated Castalla and took up a more suitable defensive posture on a hillside further north; he sent word to Mesclop (at Ibi) to send reinforcements and to the two cavalry detachments at Biar and Onil to do likewise. O'Donnell witnessed Delort's withdrawal and now found himself in a predicament; if he waited for the arrival of Santisteban's column he knew that the French force would also have received reinforcement. He therefore decided to attack and began by engaging the French cavalry, but the attacks lacked coordination and made little impression on Delort's men. A short time later, the first of the French reinforcements arrived on the scene. The 24e Dragoons thundered into General Fernando Miyares' force on the Spanish left with considerable impact but were at first checked by a hail of musket and cannon fire. The Spanish were frantically trying to organise to meet the next cavalry onslaught when Mesclop's infantry and cavalry suddenly arrived on their right. At the same time Delort ordered an all out assault on the Spanish line. O'Donnell had barely 200 cavalrymen, and they fled at the approach of the reunited cuirassiers of Mesclop and Delort.

Langlois ~ Battle of Castalla 1812
(Oil, original in Museum of Versailles, copy at the Town Hall at Castalla)

Dubessy's 24e Dragoons charged again and this time overran Miyares' line, whose right flank was in the air following the rout of the Spanish horse. The two guns up with Miyares were ridden down, having discharged only a single round apiece. Mesclop's flanking columns dislodged Michelena's Brigade from the dry river bed but his continued advance was checked by the tardy arrival of Montijo's Reserve Brigade. Delort immediately responded by sending his own escort of Dragoons around Montijo's right flank. The Badajoz Regiment, demoralized at the sight of the disaster to their front, panicked and fled at the unexpected flank attack by Delort's personal cavalry. The Regiment of Cuenca formed square and retreated in good order, but the Walloon Guards were cut off, surrounded and forced to surrender en masse. General Rafael Santisteban arrived after the fight was over and beat a hasty retreat.

The Castle at Castalla

To the east, Roche had exploited Mesclop's move in support of Delort and quickly overwhelmed the token French force left in Ibi. The advance guard under Creagh overran the dwellings but, devoid of artillery, could not take the fort and with news of Mesclop heading back to support this beleaguered group, Roche withdrew in haste. He ordered Creagh to fall back on the hills where the bulk of his Division, arms at rest, had been watching the fight for Ibi instead of following Mesclop to Castalla, as O'Donnell had instructed. Harispe's reserves finally arrived from Alcoy in the late morning and satisfied themselves with light harassment of Roche's troops as they made their way back towards Alicante. From the original Spanish force of 6,000 men, more than half were killed or captured. O'Donnell's plan was undone and in the immediate aftermath he tried to heap blame on Santisteban, claiming that he had stood idly-by as the French cavalry moved from Biar through the pass. However, in reality the Spanish Commander's plan was too fragmented and his time appreciation was flawed. On hearing the news of the disaster, Wellington was furious; O'Donnell's Army was to be out of action for many months providing Suchet badly needed time and space.

Both Naples and Sicily were *recovered* by the Spanish (having been Spanish possessions since the 13th Century) during the War of Polish Succession in 1734. The younger son of King Philip V of Spain was installed as King of Naples and Sicily a year later. After he inherited the Spanish throne from his half-brother in 1759, he established his youngest son, Ferdinand IV on the throne of the two kingdoms. Ferdinand was a member of the House of Bourbon and a natural opponent of the French Revolution and Napoleon Bonaparte. His decision to ally with the Third Coalition was, however too much for Napoleon. Following victory over the Neapolitans at Campo Tenese, Napoleon installed his older brother Joseph as King of Naples and Ferdinand fled to Sicily. Two years later Joseph was moved to Spain to assume the throne and Napoleon installed his brother in law, Marshal Joachim Murat, as King of the Two Sicilies (Sicily and Naples). Murat tried to invade Sicily on numerous occasions but failed largely due to the presence of the Royal Navy and a small British force sent to the island under Lord William Bentinck. Bentinck had orders to raise a Sicilian army of 10,000 to supplement the redcoats and it was these men who were to form the basis of the Anglo-Sicilian Expeditionary Force which landed on the east coast of Spain in mid 1812.

The Force, commanded by Lieutenant General Thomas Maitland, numbered nearly 7,000 and consisted of the 10th, 58th and 81st Regiments of Foot (first battalions), the 4th and 6th Line Battalions of the King's German Legion and parts of the foreign battalions of De Roll, Dillon and the Calabrian Free Corps. In addition, there was a squadron of the 20th Light Dragoons and Williamson's Company of the Royal Artillery. It was part of Wellington's deception operations (coordinated across Northern Spain) designed to coincide with the commencement of his Salamanca Campaign. The Anglo-Sicilian diversionary force was far weaker than Wellington had hoped and, as a result of Bentinck's vacillation, it was late on parade. It did, however, stop off en route at Minorca and Majorca to collect some more artillery and Whittingham's newly organised Balearic Division respectively. Maitland finally set sail from Palma on 28 July and arrived at Palamos, on the Catalonian coast, three days later.

Maitland's orders were to link up with General Lacy, the commander of the 1st Spanish Army, and jointly lay siege to Tarragona in order to entice Suchet's withdrawal north in support of the French Army in the region. However, Maitland appeared unconvinced that the Spanish regular and guerrilla forces in the area were up to the job; conflicting reports as to the strength of the French in the region fuelled his misgivings. When Lacy declared that he could provide little by way of provisions for the force, Maitland resolved to sail south and land at Alicante. He arrived at the port on 7 August and disembarkation commenced immediately. Roche's Division and the 67th Foot (from Cartagena) joined the Force increasing the numbers to just shy of 15,000.

Alicante, the city and the harbour were dominated by Castle Santa Barbara

The subordination of Roche's and Whittingham's Spanish divisions under overall British command is interesting as it pre-dated Wellington's appointment as *Generalissimo* of the Spanish armies in November 1812 and, as such, requires explanation. Both these divisions were financed by the British Government for 'uniforms, footwear, armaments and equipment' but their circumstances were quite different. The first of these divisions was commanded by Philip Keating Roche, an Irishman who started his military career in the Dragoon Guards and was selected to be part of the British military group despatched to assist the authorities in the Asturias at the outbreak of the Peninsular War. In 1810 he was sent to Cartagena to coordinate the maritime transport between the port and the Balearic Islands, during which he proposed to the British Ambassador (Henry Wellesley, Wellington's younger brother) that he be allowed to raise and train a Spanish division but with British funding. The concept was deemed to have merit and approved by the British and Spanish executives. He moved with his division in 1811 to Alicante, with many other formations of the Murcian Army, following the outbreak of yellow fever in and around Cartagena.

Samuel Ford (Samford) Whittingham was another fluent Spanish speaker who joined the Life Guards in 1803 and first served in Spain a year later on a secret mission for William Pitt, the Prime Minister. He took part in the ill-fated Buenos Aires operation and then moved to Gibraltar where he worked on Sir Huw Dalrymple's staff before asking to be seconded to the Spanish Army. He joined General Castaños's Army in mid 1808 and fought with La Peña's Division at Bailén. When Castaños became captain-general of Andalusia, Whittingham was appointed as the cavalry commander, promoted to major general and in 1811 took part in the Battle of Barrosa. In June that year he was sent to Majorca where he raised a cavalry corps and an officer training college. The college trained officers for his Majorca Division which numbered over 4,000 combined arms by the time that the formation joined Maitland's Anglo-Sicilian Force in July 1812.

Maitland elected to advance immediately against Suchet's two divisions and push them back north across the line of the River Xucar. However, news of the disaster at Salamanca (22 July) had already reached Suchet and he had decided to concentrate his army north of the Xucar and await the outcome of the inevitable French withdrawal in the face of Wellington's victorious Army. Maitland, meanwhile, was trying to tackle a well known Iberian dilemma: a lack of local transport and supplies. While he tried to resolve the problem, he postponed any notion of taking the offensive and merely deployed the Force to hold a line about twenty kilometres north of the city. Some British and Spanish cavalry probed the French positions on the Xucar but with events moving fast in the rest of the country, it was prudent to wait. Following Wellington's triumphant liberation of Madrid on 12 August, Joseph evacuated the city and moved east, linking up with Suchet's outposts at Almanza. His Army of the Centre numbered no more than 12,000 and consisted of the Royal Guard, D'Armagnac's Division of infantry and Treillard's Division of cavalry. Moving with this group, and numbering 3,000, was Palombini's Division (from Suchet's Army) which the King had requisitioned from Aragón in defence of the capital.

As he departed Madrid, Joseph sent orders to Soult to move with his Army of the South and concentrate around Valencia.

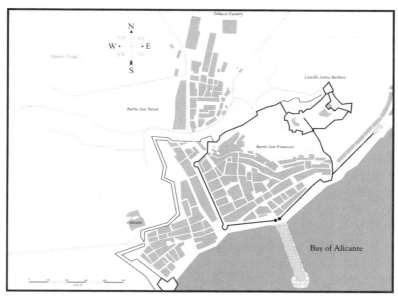

Alicante 1808 (top) and 1812 (above) depicting large scale reinforcement of the city's defences. Note the newly constructed Fort San Fernando and the levelled district of San Anton.

Rumours of Soult's evacuation of Andalusia placed the small allied concentration of the Spanish 2nd and 3rd Armies (now under General Francisco Elio's command) and that of Maitland in considerable peril. The combined armies of Joseph, Suchet and Soult would number in excess of 80,000 men. Furthermore, it was entirely conceivable that Soult would pull back and besiege both Cartagena and Alicante en route. Wellington sensed the danger and suggested Maitland concentrate in Alicante and make preparations to hold the place but to keep his transports to hand and to re-embark if the situation became critical.

Joseph Bonaparte – Napoleon's older brother (Thiers)

For the whole of September, Maitland and Elio on the one hand, and Joseph and Suchet on the other, were waiting on Soult's next move. In fact Soult had stirred as early as 17 September but, with a renewed outbreak of yellow fever at Cartagena, he had ordered the port to be given a wide berth and elected, instead, to move north via the interior. Soult arrived in the area on 2 October and the three armies were in communication. While Soult's force rested the French commanders conferred. Should they move against Wellington or strengthen their hold on the East Coast? While considering their options it came to Joseph's attention that Soult had written a despatch to the Minister of War in Paris accusing him of entering in to secret negotiations with the Spanish executive at Cadiz. It was entirely fictitious and caused considerable acrimony between the two commanders at a critical period. However, by the time they had decided upon a plan of action, news of Wellington's failure at Burgos altered the situation completely. The two armies of the Centre and South moved with speed towards Madrid forcing General Roland Hill and a number of allied divisions, in and around the capital, to retreat north. Consequently, in late October, Suchet found himself in much the same situation as the previous August.

The threat to the allied forces on the east coast diminished and on 4 December a new Spanish 2nd Army was established from the remnants of the previous 2nd and 3rd Armies. Meanwhile command of the Anglo-Sicilian Force had changed a number of times. Maitland resigned in early October from ill health and was succeeded by John Mackenzie, the senior divisional commander, who was replaced by William Clinton on 20 November. His tenure was to last only a few days, being outranked by James Campbell who arrived from Sicily with a large body of reinforcements on 2 December. He, in turn, was replaced on 25 February 1813 by Lieutenant General Sir John Murray who had been selected by Horse Guards and sent out from England.

Murray was a controversial choice for this independent command and, given his prior record, it is somewhat surprising that Wellington agreed to the appointment. Murray had served with and under Wellington on two previous occasions. In India, Murray had been the Quartermaster General from 1801 to 1805 where his inactivity was a source of great frustration to young Wellesley. But it was his behaviour in command of Wellesley's largest brigade at the recapture of Oporto in 1809 that was, perhaps, the most predictive demonstration of his abilities when entrusted with an independent mission. His failure to cut off, or even hinder, Soult's retreat from the city prompted Napier to record that *'it was an opportunity that would have tempted a blind man to strike; the neglect of it argued want of military talent and of military hardihood'*. Harsh words indeed, in fact Murray hastily departed the Iberian theatre soon after this questionable performance, but not because of it; he was concerned that he might have to serve under William Carr Beresford. This latter officer was junior in British rank to Murray but wore the rank of Marshal of the Portuguese Army, which outranked Murray in the field. Of course it must be remembered that Napier's words were penned long after the War when the full spectrum of Murray's feats were known. In contrast, Lieutenant William Woollcombe RA recorded the character of Sir John Murray, on the commander's arrival, as *'being a great martinet but a good officer'*.

A number or reinforcements had arrived from Sicily and Lisbon during the winter months, bringing the total of Murray's force up to well over 20,000 men. This included the two Spanish divisions under Whittingham and Roche, although the latter were technically part of Elio's 2nd Spanish Army. This reorganised Spanish force numbered nearly 30,000 and consisted of six divisions. Roche was with Murray's force near to Alicante and three other divisions (Villacampa, Miyares and Sarsfield) were positioned on the Murcian border about two days march from Alicante. The remaining two divisions were really groupings of the guerrilla bands of Empecinado and Duran, both of which were fundamentally operating in southern Aragón. In reality, therefore, Elio really only had about 15,000 men at his immediate disposal. Nevertheless, this provided a total force of some 35,000 against Suchet; a point the French Commander made clearly and repeatedly to Paris and Madrid at every opportunity. It was unlikely Berthier or Joseph paid much heed to Suchet's overtures for, on paper at least, his force numbered 75,000 men. However, with his extended area of operations, beset with effective guerrilla groups, and the numerous garrisons he had to maintain, his effective attacking strength on the Xucar was no more than 15,000.

Juan Martin Diez – El Empecinado
(Military Museum Burgos)

Samuel Ford Whittingham

Numbers alone, however, rarely tell the whole story. The foreign elements (Germans aside) within the Anglo-Sicilian Force were questionable indeed, consisting of (mainly) Italians but also French and Swiss deserters and a small number of Poles, Croats and the odd Dutchman. The Italians, in particular, were prone to abscond and in early February, 86 men of the 2nd Italian Levy had gone over to the French lines taking their officer with them as a prisoner. Lieutenant Woollcombe recalled a month earlier a story of nine Italians who intended to desert before meeting an Italian deserter from Suchet's army who compared their particular circumstances. He cited that in *'four years in Spain during the last two of which he received neither clothes, rations, money nor shoes, that he had been obliged to rob for his subsistence and plunder in order to obtain the common necessities in life... if under these circumstances you can conceive you can better your condition... proceed and join the army I have just left, but take the advice of an older soldier... and return with me to the English'*. Their decision is not recorded.

The questionable nature of some of his troops will have done little to inspire a naturally cautious officer like Murray but there was another impediment which complicated his taking the operational initiative. His force was almost devoid of transport: carts, wagons and the horses and mules to move them. It had been the intention to procure these resources in-country, along with the requisite provisions. However, as had been witnessed on numerous occasions by Wellington's Army in other parts of Iberia, the local military commanders were reluctant to provide either supplies or the means to transport them, for there was barely sufficient of either resource for their own indigenous purposes. Food was, accordingly, being shipped from Sicily and Algeria and a few carts and animals were procured at high prices from Spanish locals, much to the fury of authorities.

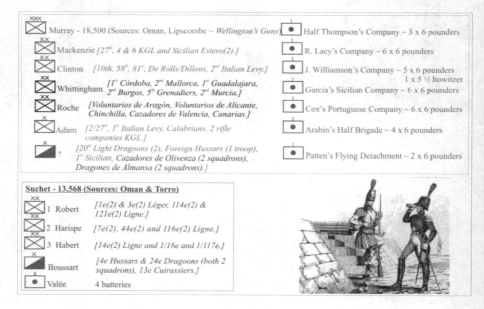

From the French perspective, operating along the coastal strip between Tortosa and Denia was not as dangerous and demanding as much of the rest of Spain. The terrain was hilly but not mountainous and did not easily facilitate guerrilla operations; indeed only one small guerrilla group under 'The Friar' (*El Fraile*) Asensio Nebot operated in the area. Nevertheless, Nebot achieved some success and Suchet offered three prisoners, who had been condemned to death, their liberty and 5,000 pesetas each if they would join Nebot's band and murder him. The three confessed on arrival at one of Nebot's hideouts and join his *partida*. The inhabitants of Valencia had not witnessed the horrors of war in quite the same way as other parts of the nation; for the most part they had not seen either British or French troops and many were uninspired by the exploits of the Spanish armies and the arrival of the Expeditionary Force. Rather than evoking insurrection there was a general apathy amongst the Valencians and a broad submission to the French yoke; a large number becoming *afrancesados* (French sympathisers).

As 1812 dawned, Suchet retained three divisions facing south; Musnier's Division (temporarily commanded by Robert) formed the right wing at Moxente; Harispe was at Xativa with a forward brigade at Alcoy; and Habert was still at Denia providing the French left wing. Murray, soon after assuming command, was apprised of the French dispositions and strengths to his front and elected to try and encircle and capture the exposed brigade at Alcoy.

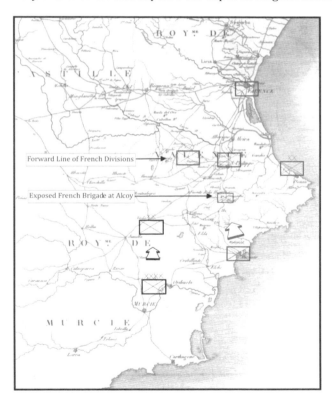

The encirclement was badly handled and the French brigade was easily able to slip away. The operation had overtones of O'Donnell's efforts the previous July; Murray's forces advancing on four separate routes with the flanking groups failed to arrive in time. Murray then dithered and after a week of doing very little he then sent Whittingham forward, unsupported, to probe the French positions at Cocentaina, a few kilometres north of Alcoy. A weak brigade, consisting of two British battalions under Major General Rufane Shaw Donkin, was sent on a left flanking manoeuvre towards Ontinyent. Suchet expected a full scale follow-up and ordered Habert to give ground. However, no additional troops were allocated to the area and no further advances were made. In fact, Murray was planning an altogether different operation; a seaborne landing of Roche's Division directly into Valencia in an attempt to capture the city. It was a bold plan which may have succeeded if executed in tandem with a land thrust of all the available Anglo-Spanish troops from the south; however, no such supporting act was contemplated and, as such, the plan was hazardous in the extreme. It is difficult to imagine how it might have succeeded. In the end, it was called off when Bentinck made noises about recalling the 6th Line KGL and some of the British grenadier companies to deal with growing problems in Sicily. A few days later, when the crisis in Sicily abated, Bentinck reversed the order. Nevertheless Murray's attack on Valencia was not reinitiated, which was undoubtedly fortuitous for at much the same time Murray received the following despatch from Wellington:

> The season is not yet sufficiently advanced to enable us here to take the field, and till we can do so in strength we should only lose the corps employed in partial attempts elsewhere. I hope soon, however, to be able to collect the army; and I shall send you instructions as to the part you are to act. I am inclined to believe that your operations must necessarily be connected with the fleet or the coast, and must be much of the same description with those carried on by me in the first campaign, that of 1808 in Portugal. There is nothing new in this part of the world.

It was early April and the combination of Wellington's and Bentinck's instructions prompted Murray to do nothing until more explicit directives should arrive. Suchet, meanwhile, was completely baffled by the actions of the forces to his front and, *ipso facto,* of Murray's and Elio's future intentions. Two isolated formations had remained inactive for nearly a month: Whittingham's north of Alcoy and Miyares' Division at Yecla. These two formations were 50 kilometres apart and 20 to 30 kilometres from the balance of the force at Castalla. Suchet recorded that he *'resolved not to wait till the forces which threatened him should be augmented or united'*. In early April he chose to strike.

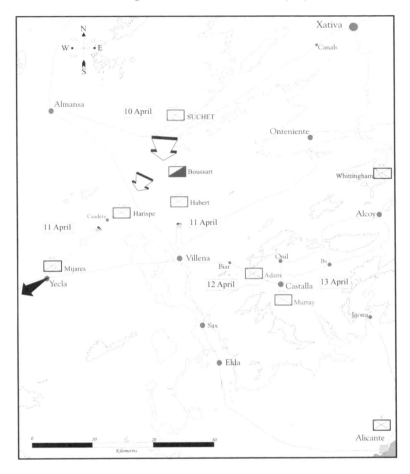

Suchet surreptitiously concentrated his strike force at Fuente la Higuera between Almansa and Xativa, leaving only a token force in front of Whittingham. Early on 10 April he advanced in two columns. Harispe's Division, supported by two cavalry regiments moved towards Miyares' Division at Yecla while the balance, led by Habert's Division, moved to capture Villena and deny any move west by Murray in support of the Spanish. It was brilliantly executed and caught both Elio and Murray off-guard. Miyares fled west towards Jumilla losing two battalions (1st Burgos and Cadiz) that were cut off while attempting to provide a rearguard. Meanwhile Habert closed on Villena where, it transpired, Elio and Murray were located having agreed to a meeting to discuss rumours of a French concentration to the north. Murray had brought Brigadier General Frederic Adam's light Brigade but wisely elected not to make a stand. Murray withdrew back to Castalla and deployed Adam in a blocking position at the Biar pass. While Elio headed south after leaving a single Spanish battalion (Vélez-Málaga) in the castle in the town, he pulled back his cavalry, deployed as a forward screen, and tried to rally the dispersed units from Miyares' Division. Habert occupied Villena without a struggle and bombarded the castle, blowing the gates on the morning of 12 April. The unfortunate Spanish commander surrendered and the battalion was lost, having been needlessly sacrificed for no tactical benefit.

Suchet's forces arrive at Biar – portrayed on the right is Adam's Brigade
(Anne S. K. Brown Military Collection, Brown University Library)

Murray recalled Whittingham from Alcoy and Roche from the south and concentrated around Castalla. Adam's men remained holding the village of Biar and the pass above. Suchet elected to drive in this Brigade and attack Murray's force on the far side. Harispe was recalled to the main body and he immediately vacated Yecla (which two of Miyares' battalions reoccupied) and moved east.   Suchet arrived in front of the town of Biar at around midday and, following a perfunctory reconnaissance, tasked Robert with the 1e Léger and the 14e Ligne and General Jean Lamarque, with the 3e Léger, the 114e and 121e Ligne, to drive in the forces in and around the town.   These consisted of the Calabrian Battalion and the light companies of the 2/27th and 3rd KGL.   The balance of the Brigade was deployed on the forward edge of the pass along with four light 4-pounder guns under Captain Arabin.

Looking west towards Biar castle from Adam's first position on the pass of Biar

The two French formations flanked the town and the allied troops fell back but the French advance was checked when it came under heavy and sustained fire from the hills above.   Suchet was irritated at this delay and hastened the infantry to reorganise for a second major attack.   The French were, once again, severely mauled as they closed in on the allied forces strung across the pass. Arabin's guns, despite only being light 4-pounders, wrecked havoc.   Suchet fed more infantry battalions into the fight until, at one stage, nine battalions were in the process of fighting to dislodge two battalions and two companies. Captain Molley was with the 2/27th and recalled the engagement.   *'The 1st and 3rd Regts of French Light Infantry en Tirailleur led the attack on our position – the left of which they turned with astonishing rapidity, whilst our whole front, and*

Right were amused by a most lively fire from the Enemy's Voltigeurs, who at the same time ascended the front; and endeavoured to gain the hills on the right on which they were anticipated by the Calabrese Light Infantry under Colonel Carey. The head of the Enemy's supporting column now shewed itself debouching from the village of Biar and was immediately cannonaded by our mountain guns'.

Two of Arabin's guns had lost their wheels while manoeuvring into position but it did not stop them firing. When the crest was vacated the guns were abandoned, the Gunners fighting them to the last before leaving them to their fate. Adam began a slow but deliberate withdrawal. He anticipated a cavalry charge, which was executed by Lieutenant Brosse of the 4e Hussars, and received a very warm reception from three skilfully deployed companies of the 2/27th which dropped a considerable number of riders from close range flanking fire as the cavalry moved down the road from the crest between the rocks. Molley recorded that *'The Line accordingly fell back slowly covered by the 8th and Light Companies of the 2/27th closely pursued by the Enemy's Light Troops; and an incessant & destructive fire was kept up on both sides... thus for 7 miles the action continued without interruption...'.* Murray had sent three battalions forward to assist the Brigade in their withdrawal in contact across the plain. About two kilometres from Castalla the relatively ineffective French pursuit was called off and Adam's men took their positions in the defensive line.

Adam's Brigade had managed to hold up Suchet's three divisions for five hours and it was late in the day when the French commander emerged from the pass. Whittingham, who witnessed the latter stages of the coordinated withdrawal, noted: *'Our advanced guard under Brigadier Adam was driven through the pass of Biar upon our main body at Castalla. But the retreat was a beautiful field-day, by alternate battalions. The volleys were admirable, and the successive passage of several ravines conducted with perfect order and steadiness. From the heights occupied by my troops it was one of the most delightful panoramas that I ever beheld!'* Indeed, the great British Peninsular War historian, Sir Charles Oman, called it one of the most creditable rearguard actions fought during the whole war. Suchet was, most certainly, having second thoughts about tackling Murray's forces now arrayed on the hillsides to the south and west of Castalla. Conscious that there were more troops to the rear and east of the feature that he could not see, he urged caution and called a halt to the day's proceedings. He ordered a full reconnaissance to be conducted and hastened the arrival of Harispe's column.

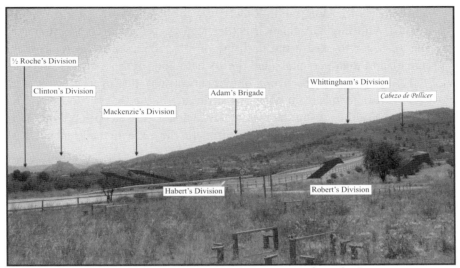

Suchet's view of the allied positions on emerging from the Biar pass

Suchet did not give his orders that evening and, uncharacteristically, took a considerable time to determine his plan of action and issue instructions the following morning. He was clearly unsure; the events of the previous day and the obvious strength of the allied positions to his front urged caution. His lieutenants, on the other hand, were quick to dispel the quality of the Spanish and Sicilian troops and advocated a rapid attack. Suchet despatched Boussart's cavalry well out to the left to reconnoitre the Castalla feature and to get an idea of the forces hidden behind the hill. Reports soon confirmed that there was a considerable body of both infantry and cavalry in reserve. In fact, behind the town of Castalla, was half of Roche's Division, the bulk of Clinton's Division (the 58th were in the castle) and the 20th Light Dragoons. To the right of the town were two well sited batteries, the other half of Roche's Division and the Spanish and Sicilian cavalry. Reports also confirmed the technical difficulty of the ground for large scale cavalry operations, the only arm with which Suchet enjoyed superiority in both numbers and ability.

Suchet's plan was quite simple. Harispe's Division, which was now up, was to remain at the Biar pass to act as a reserve, block any attempt by Elio to reinforce the allies from Sax and to protect the French line of retreat; the cavalry was to act on the French left and contain Murray's reserve; Habert was to move towards the town on the Biar - Castalla road and contain General John

Mackenzie's Division; while Robert was the main effort, on the French right, against Whittingham's Spaniards (See Map 5). At about 10 a.m. Robert moved the 1e Léger to secure the first line of hills, the Cabezo de Pellicer (modern name), and then personally led the six battalions of the 3e Léger and 114e and 121e Ligne against the strong line of skirmishers deployed in front of Adam's and Whittingham's main positions at the top of the Guerra Heights. The light troops were then given the task of advancing up the steeper hill on the French right, while the 114e were in the centre and the 121e on the French left.

The 121e being driven back at the point of the bayonet by the 2/27th Foot.
This print gives a good feel for the steepness of the terrain.
(Anne S. K. Brown Military Collection, Brown University Library)

Habert moved up the road and was soon embroiled with Mackenzie's troops. Despite Valée moving three of the French batteries to support operations in this sector, it was readily apparent that this was not going to develop into a major attack and the two commanders satisfied themselves with small scale, low-level engagements.

At the other end of the line, Whittingham found himself in a somewhat frenzied scramble to re-establish his position to meet the advance of the 3e

Léger and 114e Ligne.   Soon after Robert had commenced his advance and established the 1e Léger on the Cabezo de Pellicer, Whittingham had received an order to try and outflank the French on their extreme right.   *'About ten o'clock on the next morning, I received orders from Sir John Murray, through Lieutenant-Colonel Catanelli (an Italian officer on the staff of Lord William Bentinck) to take ground to my left till I should reach the head of a ravine in that direction, then to bring my left shoulder forwards, descending the valley, and form perpendicularly to the right of Suchet's line'.*   There is some controversy as to the source and accuracy of this order as Murray appears to have denied (to Whittingham) all knowledge about it after the affair.   Oman (*A History of the Peninsular War*) offers three possible explanations: Murray decided upon an attack early on in the day, during the long wait for Suchet's opening move, and then changed his mind; that Murray was contemplating a retreat (which is confirmed by reports of his staff) and that they initiated the order to commit him to a fight; or finally that Catanelli simply misunderstood Murray's intentions.

Whittingham had to think and act quickly.   It was fortunate that the battalions earmarked to execute the flanking manoeuvre had not moved far. His anchor battalions were able to hold the line of voltigeurs long enough to enable the flanking battalions to move to their rear and then come forward to reinforce their lines.   At several points the French reached the crest and the fighting was intense along the length of the line, but Whittingham's ability to trickle feed reserves from the back of the hill in point of fact allowed him the capacity to counter each successive French advance.   Suchet's forces had seldom met with such resistance from the Spanish throughout their long campaigning in Aragón, Catalonia and Valencia and, accordingly, it took them longer to admit defeat.   At about the same time the commanding officer of the 2/27th (Lieutenant Colonel Reeves) executed a bayonet charge on the 121e Ligne and drove them downhill.   This acted as the catalyst for Robert's other two regiments to recoil.   Suchet, positioned on top of the Cabezo de Pellicer, realised that the attack had failed; he had no intention of throwing more troops into the fray and, at about four in the afternoon, ordered a general withdrawal.

'Never perhaps during the present war was there such an opportunity as the present moment for a Commander-in-Chief to have displayed his abilities. But Sir John Murray did not take advantage of it, and surely he must have good reasons for the cautious movement which followed'.   This observation by Robert

Woollcombe was echoed in every eye-witness account of the day. He added that it was *'the received opinion of the whole army that had General Whittingham's corps advanced rapidly and turned the French right (which was easily to be done) whilst a strong column attacked them in front and the 1st [Mackenzie's] Division moved on their left, at least one half of the French army would have fallen'*. Murray did not, contrary to Woollcombe's thinking, have any good reason not to follow-up. It was, perhaps, another of Napier's circumstances that would have *'tempted a blind man to strike'*. Murray, however, refused to move until the reserve (behind Castalla) had deployed and the army had descended from the heights and paraded on the plain. By which time the French had made good their retreat. Only Habert's men were forced to fight their withdrawal as Mackenzie had ignored Murray's order and continued to press the French division to his front, as they moved back down the road towards the sanctuary of Harispe's rearguard and the defile of the Biar pass.

By the time Murray's main body advanced, the French were beyond the rearguard and the line of the French guns deployed at the mouth of the pass. Murray seemed content to make a feeble demonstration with some of the light companies before calling off the engagement. Suchet, somewhat relieved, extracted his force during the night and made best speed back to Fuente la Higuera. Arguably, Castalla was Murray's finest hour but his timidity had been apparent for all in his force to witness and did little to instill confidence in their commander. Young Woollcombe summed it up quite excellently. *'Of course during the night the whole French army retired, and the next day Sir John Murray, instead of even advancing after them at a respectful distance, marches his whole force to Alcoy. The next day he displays it in front of Puerto de Albaida, and at night retires, as readily as he had advanced, back to Alcoy. This latter movement has been wonderfully incomprehensible. Had he have marched with his army to Albaida and attacked it without waiting till the enemy were reinforced, he might have carried it, and perhaps without much loss, but even in that case it would have been useless if he had not determined to attack St. Felipe and force them across the Jucar'.*

Wonderfully incomprehensible as the follow-up may have been, the victory at Castalla was the first defeat inflicted on Suchet since Alcañiz in May 1809. Nevertheless, it did not bode well for future operations involving the Anglo-Sicilian Force while Sir John Murray's hand was on the tiller.

The day after the Battle at Castalla, and many days before Wellington had received Murray's post battle dispatch, the Commander-in-Chief penned his Memorandum for Future Operations on the East Coast – see Appendix 1. Determined not to make the same mistakes as beset the final phase of the Salamanca Campaign, Wellington planned the opening to the 1813 Campaign meticulously.   His memorandum to Murray is a good indication of the painstaking detail he applied to this operational staff work.   It is also an illuminating document in its own right.   Operations on the East Coast were undoubtedly, in Wellington's mind, integral to those of his main army; a point often overlooked by (British) historians and students of the war.   As with Bentinck's landing of the Anglo-Sicilian Force the year prior, Murray's operations were to serve as a strategic distraction to French command; however, they were also to act as the catalyst, in conjunction with the advance east from Portugal, for French evacuation of Valencia and, subsequently, Catalonia.

The Memorandum outlines three objectives: firstly, the occupation of the region of Valencia; secondly, the establishment of a presence on the coast north of the Ebro; thirdly, thereby the northerly withdrawal of the French from the lower Ebro. Wellington provides Murray the flexibility to achieve objective 2 in advance of objective 1, but he also caveats that 'I shall forgive any thing [*sic*], excepting that one of the corps should be beaten or dispersed'. This laid the seeds of failure. It requires a commander of great ability and audaciousness to be able to operate with his back to the sea and with the enemy on the other three sides.   Murray, as we have seen, was not the greatest tactician; as to boldness and daring, there was, perhaps, not a weaker or more indecisive general in the whole Wellington's Peninsular Army.

The Memorandum is also very specific concerning coalition operations with the Spanish (regular and irregular) forces.   Translated copies of the Memorandum were sent to General Ramon Copons (1st Army in Catalonia), General Elio (2nd Army) and the Duque del Parque (3rd Army – an amalgamation of the old Army of Centre and elements of Army of Estremadura).   Of the irregular forces, José Duran (in concert with General Pedro Villacampa) was to prevent communication between Joseph and Suchet, while El Empecinado was held in reserve for tasking as operations unfolded. Whittingham's and Roche's Divisions were, once again, task organised under Murray's command but Wellington, in a private letter to Murray accompanying the Memorandum, was quite clear that they were not to be resupplied from British sources. Wellington had, by this time, been stripped of his title and role as *Generalissimo* of the Spanish Army and although the Campaign of 1813 had been planned and was executed in conjunction with the Spanish allies, he still held considerable reservations as to their strategic and operational reliability. In the same letter he outlined these concerns to Murray. *'In forming a plan of operations for [Spanish] troops in the Peninsula, it is necessary always to bear in mind their inefficiency, notwithstanding their good inclinations, their total want of every thing [sic] which could keep them together as armies, and of the necessary equipments of cannon, &c. &c., and their repeated failures in the accomplishment even of the most trifling objects, notwithstanding the personal bravery of the individuals composing the armies. If I had had to form a plan for the operations of half the numbers, real soldiers, well equipped and prepared for the field, it would have been one of a very different description ; but such a plan would not suit, and could not be executed by the instruments with which you have to work'.*

All operations on the east coast were intrinsically linked to the Royal Navy and were, *ipso facto*, truly joint. The Royal Navy had brought the force to the Levant and now played a major role in maintaining it and in facilitating plans for future operations. The Royal Navy had been pivotal to operations up and down the coast since the beginning of the War; their contribution being far more than merely transporting forces and supplies. The Commander of the Mediterranean Fleet, Admiral Sir Edward Pellew, had tasked Rear Admiral Hallowell in early 1812 to conduct a thorough reconnaissance along the east coast and it had been on Hallowell's submission that the initial landing site of the Anglo-Sicilian Force was to be at Palamos. Hallowell had responsibility to transport the Force in July and, following disembarkation at Alicante, he remained with the 65 transports in the safe anchorage provided by the port. Thus retaining the operational mobility of the force and the means to harass Suchet's Army almost at will.

In August 1812 two gunships (*Fame and Termagant*) sailed up the coast with the 18-gun sloop *Philomel* and destroyed the evacuated French coastal batteries and strong points at Villajoyosa, Benidorm, Altea and Calpe. Later the

Fame engaged French forces at Denia and anchored at Javea Bay, providing support to the locals there before being driven back on board by Habert's infantry, leaving the locals to face the inevitable French reprisals. In October, the *Fame* returned with the 18-gun sloop *Cephalus* and 600 troops to Denia in an attempt to take the Fort by *coup de main*. They failed but the *Minstrel* had succeeded in September in capturing four French vessels moving ammunition to Peñiscola. As demoralising as these attacks were to the French, it was the Royal Navy's ability to resupply, with impunity, the Spanish regular and irregular forces, particularly in Catalonia, which had the greatest impact on the war in the region. Between May and November 1812 they had supplied over 4,500 muskets, along with numerous pistols and bayonets, and over 300,000 cartridges to the Catalans. The French enjoyed no such facility; indeed the sheer presence of the Royal Navy, and their virtual sea supremacy, actively denied the French the ability to move troops and be resupplied by sea through a series of successful (and some less successful) blockading operations up and down the coast.

Pellew's instructions to Hallowell, to remain in direct support of the Anglo-Sicilian Force, accounts for the lack of correspondence from Wellington to Pellew, the Admiralty or Earl Bathurst (the Secretary of War) on the matter of naval transports for the Tarragona operation. It also explains why his Memorandum is somewhat vague over the capacity of the transport fleet as this was something he expected Murray to negotiate with Hallowell directly.

Tarragona Fort and harbour and Fort Olivo in the foreground

A number of reinforcements had arrived since The Battle at Castalla and Murray's force now amounted to more than 21,000 men. Over 16,000 embarked on 31 May, destined for the Catalonian coast. Elio's troops filled the positions vacated by the Anglo-Sicilians and Whittingham's Division, while those of the Duque Del Parque moved from the border region of Andalusia and deployed into the areas around Yecla and Chinchilla as Elio's men moved forward. These two armies, numbered 40,000 and were fully armed, resupplied and poised to advance at the first sign that the French line to their front was weakening.

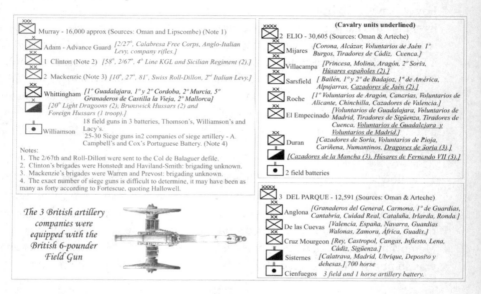

Murray - 16,000 approx (Sources: Oman and Lipscombe) (Note 1)

Adam - Advance Guard *[2/27", Calabresa Free Corps, Anglo-Italian Levy, company rifles.]*

1 Clinton (Note 2) *[58", 2/67", 4" Line KGL and Sicilian Regiment (2).]*

2 Mackenzie (Note 3) *[10", 27", 81", Swiss Roll-Dillon, 2" Italian Levy.]*

Whittingham *[1" Guadalajara, 1"y 2" Cordoba, 2"Murcia, 5" Granaderos de Castilla la Vieja, 2" Mallorca]*
[20" Light Dragoons (2), Brunswick Hussars (2) and Foreign Hussars (1 troop).]

Williamson 18 field guns in 3 batteries, Thomson's, Williamson's and Lacy's.
25-30 Siege guns in2 companies of siege artillery - A. Campbell's and Cox's Portuguese Battery. (Note 4)

Notes:
1. The 2/67th and Roll-Dillon were sent to the Col de Balaguer defile.
2. Clinton's brigades were Honstedt and Haviland-Smith: brigading unknown.
3. Mackenzie's brigades were Warren and Prevost: brigading unknown.
4. The exact number of siege guns is difficult to determine, it may have been as many as forty according to Fortescue, quoting Hallowell.

The 3 British artillery companies were equipped with the British 6-pounder Field Gun

(Cavalry units underlined)

2 ELIO - 30,605 (Sources: Oman & Arteche)

Mijares *[Corona, Alcázar, Voluntarios de Jaén 1° Burgos, Tiradores de Cádiz, Cuenca.]*

Villacampa *[Princesa, Molina, Aragón, 2° Soria, Húsares españoles (2).]*

Sarsfield *[Bailén, 1"y 2° de Badajoz, 1° de América, Alpujarras, Cazadores de Jaén (2).]*

Roche *[1° Voluntarios de Aragón, Canarias, Voluntarios de Alicante, Chinchilla, Cazadores de Valencia.]*

El Empecinado *[Voluntarios de Guadalajara, Voluntarios de Madrid, Tiradores de Sigüenza, Tiradores de Cuenca, Voluntarios de Guadalajara y Voluntarios de Madrid.]*

Duran *[Cazadores de Soria, Voluntarios de Rioja, Cariñena, Numantinos, Dragones de Soria (3).]*

[Cazadores de la Mancha (3), Húsares de Fernando VII (3).]

2 field batteries

3 DEL PARQUE - 12,591 (Sources: Oman & Arteche)

Anglona *[Granaderos del General, Carmona, 1° de Guardias, Cantabria, Cuidad Real, Cataluña, Irlanda, Ronda.]*

De las Cuevas *[Valencia, España, Navarra, Guardias Walonas, Zamora, África, Guadix.]*

Cruz Mourgeon *[Rey, Castropol, Cangas, Infiesto, Lena, Cádiz, Sigüenza.]*

Sisternes *[Calatrava, Madrid, Ubrique, Deposito y dehesas.] 700 horse*

Cienfuegos *3 field and 1 horse artillery battery.*

Suchet was well aware of the allied preparations and his brigade sized reaction force, under General Claude Pannetier, monitored and shadowed the fleet as it sailed up the coast past his initial positions at Valencia. They were, however, unsure of its intended destination. Suspicions that the target was to be Tarragona were confirmed on 2 June when the fleet sheltered under the lee of Cape Salou, eight nautical miles south of the city.

Copons (1st Army) met with Murray and, despite reservations, agreed to concentrate about twelve battalions, and some cavalry, sixteen kilometers west of Tarragona. This constituted all the available troops of his Army, as the balance of 15,000 men were required to hold the garrisons in the interior; a problem not exclusive to the French. Two of these battalions were earmarked to join a small force (2/67th and De Roll-Dillon's Battalion), tasked by Murray, to move under Colonel Prevost directly to the Col-de-Balaguer where they were to take control of the defile and capture the small Fort of San Filipe located there. This was a sensible precaution as the defile controlled the coast road from the lower Ebro, the only road suitable for artillery. Capture of the Fort was, in Murray's orders, 'desirable' but as the structure dominated the defile it is difficult to imagine how Prevost would deny the road without having possession of it. In fact, aided by the Royal Navy, it took Prevost's men four days to bring the small French garrison (a company with twelve guns) to its knees. In the end, it was a chance round from one of the mortars landed by Captain Peyton RN, aboard the *Stromboli*, which ignited one of the Fort's magazines, prompting the commander to surrender. It was in Prevost's hands by nightfall on 7 June.

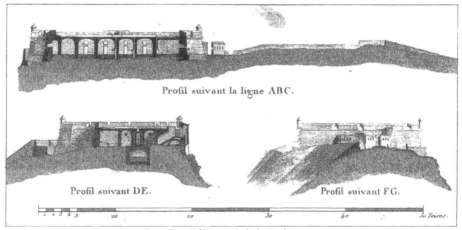

Fort San Filipe at Col-de-Balaguer

At Salou Bay the force began disembarkation early on the 3rd June and by mid afternoon the entire force and twenty two guns (a mix of field and siege) had been brought ashore. The investment of Tarragona, under Donkin (Murray's chief of staff), was complete that night. Murray conducted a reconnaissance of the place with his Chief Engineer, Major Thackeray, and his Commander Royal Artillery, Major Williamson, and they concluded, not surprisingly, that an attack from the west was the best option. Two batteries (1 and 2) were marked out and work began immediately on the positions adjacent to the road running parallel to the Francoli River. Tom Scott, the Brigade Major to the CRA, noted on 5 June that: *'this day we made some advance and in the evening threw four 8-*

in Howitzers into a battery on the sea beach, about 900 yards from the body of the place and another battery of two 24s near the main road'.

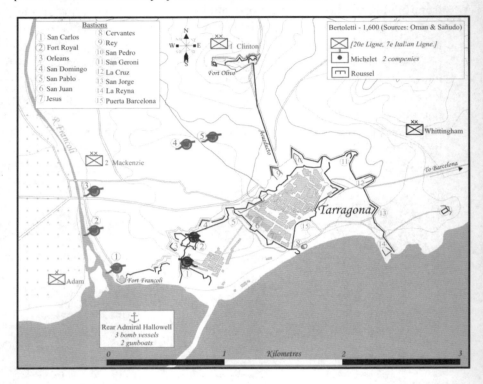

To General Antoine Bertoletti and his small French garrison, the sight of this large besieging force, complete with a number of siege guns, immediately sapped their morale and fostered a feeling of hopelessness. It was an inadequate garrison force but under the circumstances it was the best Suchet could furnish. Bertoletti did his best to raise the spirits of his men, unaware at this stage that his best ally was in fact the Allied Commander himself. Murray had, as early as 3 June, developed a fixation of hopelessness about the mission. He was convinced that the fortress was invincible and that a combined army of 25,000 men, Decaen from the north and Suchet from the south, were poised to simultaneously fall on his force. Hallowell, Clinton and Mackenzie were beside themselves with anger at the way the siege was being conducted and by the way Murray kept them all in the dark with regard to his intentions. They all considered the lower defences in the town assailable by escalade but Murray was having none of it.

On the 7th June Thackeray reported that the outworks were ready for an assault but added, strangely, that *'if the fort were escaladed and occupied, the ground gained would be of no immediate use for the attack upon the Upper city, whose most accessible front might be more easily battered from the slopes of the Olivo hill'.* Based on this extraordinary analysis, Murray decided to defer the attack and open two new batteries on the Olivo Hill. This decision was all the more astonishing as Murray had received confirmation that day of Prevost's success at Col-de-Balaguer. He had every reason to be pleased with progress and optimistic of the outcome, instead he penned a note to Wellington in which he wrote that *'I am much afraid we have undertaken more than we are able to perform'.* He began to express these concerns more openly and talked of lifting the siege and embarking the force but he seemed to shy away from the idea when discussions with Hallowell manifested the naval officer's unbridled disgust at the proposal.

More guns and siege stores were landed and hauled into place. Many had to be manhandled due to the lack of transport and, in the interim, Hallowell's naval guns continued to bombard the town to keep the heads of the defenders down and disrupt their deadly counter fire. Within two days these two additional batteries (4 and 5) were ready; they opened on 10 June and by the next day had battered a suitable breach. Orders were given to Clinton to execute an attack that night and Murray set off to Copons' (new) headquarters amidst rumours that a force of 10,000 men (under General David Maurice Mathieu) was moving south from Barcelona. Copons had moved his force to counter and at the subsequent meeting Murray promised the Spanish commander considerable reinforcements. On returning to Tarragona, Murray received news that Suchet was at Perello, about 50 kilometres from the city and on the far side of the defile of Col-de-Balaguer. This frankly insignificant intelligence was the tipping-point for Murray who lost his composure completely. Wellington's warning that *'the one thing that could not be forgiven would be that the corps should be beaten or dispersed'* echoed in his mind. He delayed the assault and then cancelled it and then he called off the siege and ordered the force to embark by dusk on 12 June.

Protestations from Hallowell and Williamson bought more time and a delegation of generals, including Mackenzie, Adam and Donkin, tried to convince Murray to put the siege on hold and advance north to defeat the French force but Murray, his mind in turmoil but made up, came up with all manner of reasons as to why such a scheme would open the door for Suchet to attack from the south. At 10 a.m. on 12 June, news that Maurice Mathieu's column was a few hours march from the city induced another extraordinary set of orders and subsequent counter-orders from Murray. The infantry were to be got off at all costs, horses and mules might have to be shot and food and ammunition abandoned. Hallowell refused to comply and ordered the animals and stores brought aboard and he delayed departure until sometime after sunrise on 13 June. However, the siege guns in the Olivo batteries could not be moved and eighteen pieces were spiked in situ.

Worst of all Copons was left stranded; having reneged on his promises of support, Murray left the unfortunate Spanish commander no choice but to withdraw. The force embarked and was away from the shore when Murray then asked Hallowell to land three battalions near the Col-de-Balaguer to assist in the extraction of Prevost's detachment. They were landed late on 13 June. The next day Suchet came up from the south and reconnoitred the defile; he was extremely concerned to see it in the hands of a considerable British force. As Suchet pondered, news arrived informing him that two Spanish armies had attacked Harispe and Habert and were threatening Valencia. Murray seemed to sense the opportunity and, in an attempt to make amends for his behaviour at Tarragona, suggested a large-scale landing to isolate and capture Pannetier's Brigade, which had taken an interior road and was, by now, badly isolated.

On 15 June the entire force was once again disembarked but by the time they had organised themselves and tried to procure some mules and carts, Pannetier had withdrawn and linked up with Suchet's main force. Over the next two days Murray was convinced that Suchet was about to attack and implored support from Copons. The Spanish commander agreed, but then changed his mind as reports arrived that Maurice Mathieu's force was once again closing on Tarragona from the north. Copons repositioned his infantry to engage the advancing French in the flank. It was a bold action as the two groups were numerically balanced but Copons had fewer cavalry and no artillery. In the end, the Spanish were once again forced to withdraw the following day because of Murray's inactivity.

On the morning of 17 June Murray was again in a state of uncertainty and nervous vacillation. He held a council of war, as is the want of a man devoid of ideas and a decisive mind, and his generals advised him to re-embark the force. The loading began later that day and continued until the very early hours of the 19 June bringing an end to the tribulations of the force but not to this woeful tale. Following a letter from Hallowell to Pellew, British Ministers gave orders on 14 July that Murray should be tried by Court Martial in Spain. This was a commitment Wellington could have done without as operations in northern Spain, following the dramatic victory at Vitoria on 21st June, were all consuming and continuing apace. In the end Murray was brought to trial in Winchester in January 1815. Fortsecue (*History of the British Army*) maintains the prosecution was 'unskilfully conducted' and Murray was acquitted of all charges but found guilty of an error in judgement by unnecessarily abandoning his guns and stores at Tarragona. Fortescue closes his chapter with a damning indictment, writing that Murray *'must be pilloried by history without mercy as a cowardly and dishonourable man, unworthy to hold his Sovereign's Commission or to wear the red coat of a British soldier'*. Many members of his force would undoubtedly have agreed.

Lieutenant General Sir John Murray
(Private Collection)

Bentinck, who had (sometime earlier) been ordered to assume command of the Force, had departed Sicily with great reluctance and arrived on Pellew's flagship on 18 June. Having been fully apprised of the less than satisfactory situation, he hastened his landing at the Col-de-Balaguer and relieved Murray of command. Bentinck ordered the fort to be blown up, as he had no intention of garrisoning it; the following day, as soon as the fleet was ready, it set sail for Alicante. An angry north-easterly caused considerable problems driving fourteen of the transports onto the sandy estuary of the Ebro: four could not be refloated and had to be burned once their consignments had been re-loaded on other ships. This caused frustrating delays and the fleet arrived back at Alicante in dribs and drabs over the period 22 to 26 June.

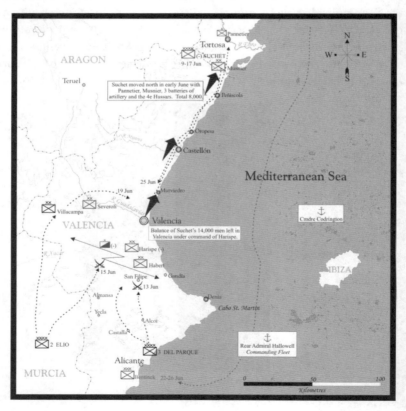

Bentinck was less than enamoured by circumstances as he found them. The attack by the Spanish 2nd and 3rd Armies on the French forces left in the region had failed. On paper the Spanish outnumbered the French threefold (see page 72) but in reality the available numbers were nearer double the opposition, with Elio having only a direct hand on about 20,000 of his charge. Wellington's Memorandum had left clear directions as to the employment of these armies once Suchet headed north: *'the third army of the Duque del Parque should be employed to turn the right of the enemy's positions in Valencia, while the allied troops under Sir John Murray and General Elio will attack them in front'*. Wellington had chosen Del Parque's Army for the more difficult manoeuvre operation as he considered these troops (after those of Copons) to be the best Spanish troops in all their armies. However, for reasons unknown, Elio had convinced Del Parque to switch roles; their combined advance commencing on 9 June, some days after Suchet's departure.

In the end it was Del Parque's frontal assault on the bridgeheads along the Xucar that was to misfire. Advancing on two routes, on a wide front and on roads which lacked lateral communication and mutual support, his forces were divided. Harispe pounced on 13 June against the easterly column at Carcagente and routed three Spanish brigades; Del Parque was with the other half of his force but unable to move to support them. With his Army's capability badly affected by the setback, he elected to withdraw and wait for the outcome of Elio's wide, left flanking manoeuvre, which was being executed by Villacampa's Division. As it transpired, this too came to nothing. By the time Villacampa had bypassed Severoli's Italian Division and reached the main Madrid – Valencia road and swung east, intelligence reported that Suchet's forces were rapidly returning from the north. (Suchet had departed on the night of 17 June after witnessing the destruction of Fort San Filipe and arrived back in Valencia on 25 June). Villacampa delayed overly long and was eventually chased into the interior by Musnier's Division as they debouched into the plains beneath Saguntum Fort.

Bentinck, keen to kick start operations was, however, facing other problems. Murray, when he departed for Tarragona and against Wellington's unequivocal instruction, had released the mules and carts constituting the Force's land transport. But any hope of salvaging something from the month of June was dealt a terminal blow following his visit, a few days later, to the Spanish units in the field. Del Parque's demoralised force was a particular concern. He wrote to

Wellington. *'If your Lordship could see this Spanish Army, I think you would be of the opinion that alone, and not supported by troops in whom they have more confidence than in themselves, they are good for little or nothing'.* Nevertheless, Bentinck discussed options with both Elio and Del Parque and they fashioned a plan which involved the Anglo-Sicilian Force and Del Parque's Army executing a (somewhat half-baked) wide westerly flanking manoeuvre around Suchet's line on the Xucar, while Elio held their attention from the south. Suchet conversely, having repositioned his forces, was poised to resume the offensive and he had Del Parque's battered force firmly in his sights. However, before long news of the catastrophic defeat on the French at Vitoria reached the east coast commanders and everything changed.

Bentinck received the news days before Suchet: the guerrillas had intercepted most of the French communiqués since the start of the Vitoria Campaign. In fact, Suchet had been growing increasingly anxious throughout June with reports, albeit sporadic, of Joseph's combined armies withdrawing north-eastwards at an alarming rate. However, when confirmation of the disaster arrived at his headquarters at Valencia on 3 July, Suchet wasted no time in issuing immediate orders to his forces to evacuate Valencia and move north of the Ebro. The report had come from Suchet's commander at Saragossa, General Paris, who informed him that Clausel had fallen back on the city having failed to link up with Joseph's combined armies in time for the battle at Vitoria. Suchet's aim was now to join forces with Clausel and then move on Wellington's flank. He departed Valencia on 5 July and reached the south bank of the Ebro four days later. The French troops were well disciplined on the march and received an uninterrupted passage from the locals and guerrillas as their reward. It had been a textbook withdrawal except for one undisputed error. Suchet had left a single company in Denia, two battalions in Saguntum and another in Peñiscola. This policy only served to reduce the strength of his Army at a critical juncture in the campaign; it was a flawed strategy which, uncharacteristically, he was to continue to adopt in the months ahead.

In Catalonia, following Murray's departure, Copons had withdrawn back to his mountain hideouts and Decaen had planned and commenced an operation to flush them out. When he received the news of Vitoria he tried to recall General Isidore Lamarque, commanding the strike force, but he was already locked in minor skirmishes with Baron d'Eroles' Division and did not receive the order to return to Gerona. Copons had been monitoring Lamarque's advance and sent an additional brigade to assist Eroles; the French column would have been destroyed had Decaen not sent Beurmann's Brigade to the rescue. They arrived just in time; Lamarque had lost 400 men (including 31 of his officers) his musket ammunition was all but spent and that of his artillery expended. The upshot of this unfortunate debacle was notification from Marshal Berthier that Decaen had became the fifth French commander in Catalonia to be replaced. In fact, he remained in country and was succeeded by Suchet.

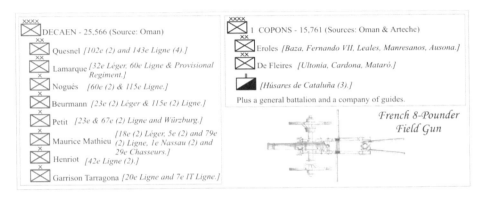

DECAEN - 25,566 (Source: Oman)

Quesnel *[102e (2) and 143e Ligne (4).]*

Lamarque *[32e Léger, 60e Ligne & Provisional Regiment.]*

Nogués *[60e (2) & 115e Ligne.]*

Beurmann *[23e (2) Léger & 115e (2) Ligne.]*

Petit *[23e & 67e (2) Ligne and Würzburg.]*

Maurice Mathieu *[18e (2) Léger, 5e (2) and 79e (2) Ligne, 1e Nassau (2) and 29e Chasseurs.]*

Henriot *[42e Ligne (2).]*

Garrison Tarragona *[20e Ligne and 7e IT Ligne.]*

1 COPONS - 15,761 (Sources: Oman & Arteche)

Eroles *[Baza, Fernando VII, Leales, Manresanos, Ausona.]*

De Fleires *[Ultonia, Cardona, Mataró.]*

[Húsares de Cataluña (3).]

Plus a general battalion and a company of guides.

French 8-Pounder Field Gun

On 9 July as Suchet arrived at Tortosa he received a despatch from Clausel informing him that the latter commander had elected to head for the pass at Jaca, cross the Pyrenees and rejoin Joseph's Army. The possibility of a link-up had therefore passed and Suchet sent orders to General Paris at Saragossa, to march immediately to Mequinenza and rejoin the main body of Suchet's Army. However, Paris did not receive the order before he had been driven out of Saragossa by Duran's (irregular) Division. The strong and capable *ad hoc* group of irregulars, which included some very capable cavalry units under Julian Sanchez and Mina, got ahead of Paris's formation as it headed east and drove it north. Paris decided to escape over the pass at Jaca, following in Clausel's footsteps. Suchet received the disappointing news on 14 July and decided to pull back to Catalonia, where he established his headquarters at Tarragona. Robert was left to garrison Tortosa with nearly 5,000 men; Lamarque was sent to Lerida with 2,000 (replacing the ailing Henriot) and a battalion was despatched to Mequinenza. To be exact, these locations already had garrisons, Suchet merely enhanced their strengths but, in so doing, he frittered away a further 3,000 men from his main army. He did, however, assume full command of the Army of Catalonia and so received another 25,000 men. His first task for

Decaen, now his second in command, was to organise and field a force of 10,000 of his subordinated Army to join his active field force against the inevitable allied attack from the south.

Bentinck did his utmost to speed the 'inevitable' attack but it was not until 9 July that the advance guard entered Valencia, with the two Spanish armies still a few days march behind. Bentinck drew up a detailed plan of action with Elio and Del Parque on 13 July. Elio was to engage the French garrisons in the region and man and repair the city of Valencia with his Army, less Villacampa's Division, which was to join the Anglo-Sicilian Force with Del Parque's Army and head north. Bentinck's force set off from Valencia on 16 July with the Spanish still some days behind. Lacking up to date intelligence from Wellington and convinced that Suchet was about to quit Catalonia, Bentinck opted for a second amphibious assault on Tarragona.

Following reports of Clausel's withdrawal to France, the loss of Paris's strong Brigade and unaware that Joseph had been replaced by Soult (on 12 July) Suchet considered his options for his substantial force of more than 50,000 men. He could move on Wellington's extended right flank; he could withdraw back to France and move to support the main army; he could withdraw to northern Catatonia behind the River Llobregat; or he could defend as far forward as necessary to retain access to the Ebro valley and his garrisons at Lérida and Tortosa. Not surprisingly, given the large numbers of troops he had ensconced in the various garrisons throughout Aragón, Valencia and Catalonia, he elected for the latter option. His loss of Aragón was considered an irreparable misfortune but his greatest concern was that Wellington would detach a force down the Ebro valley to link up with Bentinck and the Spanish. In fact, although Suchet's decision was about to wrong-foot Bentinck, it played directly into Wellington's hands. For the arrival of another 50,000 men on the Western Pyrenees, to supplement the 80,000 of Soult's Army would, almost certainly have derailed Wellington's planned invasion of France.

On 21 July Clinton's Division was loaded onto transports, which were called forward from Alicante, pre-loaded with the artillery train and siege supplies, and moved to Tarragona in the hope of taking control of the city which, according to recent accounts, had been abandoned by the French. Clinton arrived in Tarragona Bay three days later and observed a number of French baggage trains heading north but also large numbers of French soldiers and Spanish civilians working to repair the bastions. Meanwhile, Bentinck had crossed the Ebro at Amposta and was heading north with his force (less Clinton's Division) and Whittingham's Spaniards. It took several days for this force to reach the Col-de-Balaguer where Clinton's Division rejoined them from the sea, bringing Bentinck's numbers to 16,000. Del Parque's Army and Villacampa's Division were still some days to the south. On 30 July Bentinck advanced towards Tarragona unaware of just how precarious his situation was.

Suchet, lacking accurate intelligence, took Bentinck's advance as indicative of far greater strength and awaited Decaen's arrival before considering his options, ever conscious of Copons' force on his right flank. Bentinck sited his force at Tarragona and waited a full two weeks for all the Spanish forces to close-up. When they did arrive, it was impossible to keep them concentrated as there were insufficient resources to sustain so many men in such a confined area. Bentinck, well aware of Wellington's stinging rebuke to Murray about the loss of the siege guns, considered it prudent to delay the landing of the siege train. Copons, meanwhile, was still smarting from Murray's behaviour in June and loath to commit to combined operations under Bentinck. While the allies dithered, Suchet struck. On 14 August he advanced with four divisions; two against Whittingham, covering the inland passes, and the other two against Bentinck at Tarragona. Both fell back to the Col-de-Balaguer where Suchet found them on 17 August in a strong position and therefore declined to attack.

Leaving a cavalry screen to cover the allies, Suchet withdrew back to Tarragona where he carried out his initial intention to evacuate and destroy the city. The bastions were blown and Decaen's two divisions were sent back north, fuelling renewed rumours that Suchet was poised to evacuate Spain. Bentinck, concerned that this signalled the French marshal's intent to march in support of Soult, and conscious of Wellington's instructions to try to prevent such a union, despatched Del Parque to Tudela. This action merely served to reduce Bentinck's numbers, and his options, in the weeks ahead. In fact, Del Parque's Army was to play no further part in the war, only one of its divisions being called forward to assist in the blockade of Pamplona. Despite repeated appeals by Soult for Suchet to march his considerable forces west in the defence of France, Suchet chose to ignore his colleague. He had decided that, short of a direct order from the Emperor himself, he would remain in Catalonia protecting the eastern approaches. With Napoleon embroiled in events in central Europe, he calculated that such a notification would be long in arriving.

Despite good intelligence that Suchet had indeed evacuated Tarragona and headed north, Bentinck remained cautious and did not resume his advance until late August. By 29 August he was at Tarragona and making plans for the repair of the main fort and for improvements to the port for use as a naval base and logistic hub. Copons paid him a flying visit and plans were drawn up for a combined operation against the French at Barcelona. Of his original force, formations were widely spread: Del Parque had long departed; Villacampa was observing Tortosa; Duran's Division was blockading Lérida and Mequinenza; El Empecinado's was near Madrid; and the two divisions from Elio's Army, Roche and Miyares, were besieging Saguntum and Peñiscola respectively. Only

Whittingham's and Sarsfield's divisions were therefore available for the subsequent offensive.

On 5 September Bentinck left Tarragona with only 12,000 men of the Anglo-Sicilian Force having decided to leave the two Spanish Divisions in and around Tarragona for want of provisions and transport. Frederick Adam, commanding the advance guard, was ordered to occupy the defile at Ordal on the morning of 12 September. Adam's group numbered just over 1,500 men and four 6-pounder guns. Bentinck accompanied Adam and conducted a reconnaissance of the position; he personally deployed the forces utilising the three old, and largely ruined, trenched redoubts that spanned the road. Later that afternoon, the leading brigade of Pedro Sarsfield's Division came up; it is unclear whether this reinforcement was planned or happenstance. Either way, their arrival provided another 2,300 troops and Adam adjusted his deployment accordingly.

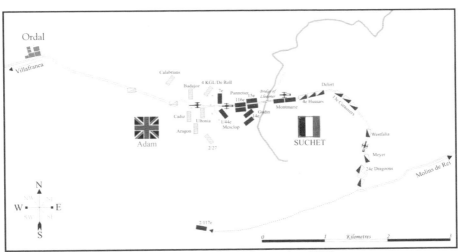

The Combat at Ordal, 13 September 1813

Inexplicably neither the cavalry, nor an infantry picket, were sent forward to cover the significant defile and bridge a few hundred metres to their front. Suchet, having gathered a sizable force of nearly 20,000 men, decided to seize the pass in a night operation and then link up with Decaen's column (which constituted 7,000 of this number) and descend on Bentinck's Force at Villafranca. It was a risky operation and a difficult approach as the precipitous terrain dictated an advance in Indian file, a condition which prevented the attacker deploying his force and considerably aided the defender. Suchet took the risk, crossed the bridge without a shot being fired and surprised the defenders. A fierce firefight ensued, lighting up the hillsides with the profuse small-arms' discharges. The defenders were quickly overwhelmed and, as they struggled to remove the guns, their positions were turned and they fled in disorder down the track towards Villafranca.

The Cross at the Col de Ordal

Suchet allowed his exhausted men some rest before pursuing the small force. At Villafranca he found Bentinck arrayed in a good defensive position on the outskirts of the town. There was no sign of Decaen, who had been embroiled in chasing off the Calabrese Free Corps which had stumbled upon the French column in their attempt to escape, across the hills, from the attack at Ordal. Suchet decided to wait and Bentinck used the lull to instigate an orderly withdrawal. After a brief but furious cavalry engagement Bentinck's force pulled back to Tarragona, stopping twice en route to thwart Suchet's spirited chase. This rather unsatisfactory affair brought to an end, large-scale combat operations on the east coast. Suchet withdrew and dispersed his army and Bentinck returned to Sicily, handing over command to General William Clinton, the senior divisional commander who Wellington was to later say 'Did nothing in particular – and did it pretty well'.

In November Suchet received instruction from Napoleon to abandon the Ebro fortresses, which were destroyed on evacuation. He then concentrated his Army around Barcelona but decided to make one last attack on the Anglo-Sicilian Force and drive it back beyond the Ebro; it failed completely. Suchet's last few months in 1813 were taken up with Napoleon's Treaty of Valençay (the name of Count Talleyrand's château where Ferdinand VII had been held in captivity since 1808) which cited the release of Ferdinand VII and a peace between France and Spain. This optimistic plan would, in Napoleon's opinion, enable the French garrisons along the east coast to march unhindered back to join Suchet who, in turn, could be used to influence events in eastern France or join Soult and thwart Wellington's future attentions in the south of that country. Suchet received orders from Paris in early January 1814 to prepare for his withdrawal from Spain. He was delighted at the prospect of vacating Catalonia and joining the Emperor on operations in the defence of France; it had been many years since he had served directly under Napoleon. He complied with the order but within weeks it was apparent that the Treaty of Valençay had failed and the Catalan forces moved against the remnants of his force with a renewed vigour.

Clinton moved the Anglo-Sicilians north to conduct combined operations with Copons against Barcelona. These were mistimed and Clinton was compelled to withdraw after his force was discovered. It was the last operation the Anglo-Sicilians were to fight in the Battle for the East Coast; Wellington sent orders to break up the Corps on 10 March. Suchet's last few months were entangled with a series of intrigues, in escorting Ferdinand VII to Madrid and in sending yet more troops back to France. News of Napoleon's abdication at the end of March and of the final Battle at Toulouse on 10 April reached Barcelona on 18 April, two days after Habert's desperate sortie – as it turned out this was to be the last action of the Peninsular War.

Barcelona, Fort Monjuic in the distance (Hugo)

The British Military General Service Medal, when it was issued in 1847, had twenty-one Peninsular War battle or campaign clasps. None were for service on the east coast - Wellington's Forgotten Front. But the east coast was not forgotten by Wellington, quite the contrary, and it was most certainly not a forgotten front to the French or Spanish. It is curious that service in this theatre of operations was overlooked or not considered suitably meritorious for recognition by the British establishment. It is also interesting that eyewitness accounts and primary sources are so few and far between for the participants and veterans of the east coast. It is, perhaps, a combination of these two points which have led to a number of recent studies of the War which, at best, have brushed over the campaign on the east coast and, at worst, ignored it altogether.

In many aspects, the East Coast theatre was to Joseph, what the Iberian ulcer was to Napoleon. The operational theatre's proximity to the coast, the naval supremacy enjoyed by the Royal Navy and the inevitable link between these two factors make it a truly joint campaign. Ignoring the east coast was not an option for any of the protagonists. To the Spanish, the east coast was a matter of national survival; the ports of Valencia, Alicante and Cartagena sustained the nation, fed the people and greased the military machine. To Wellington, the east coast was a necessary and cost effective distraction but, by 1812, it had become an integral component of the allied campaigns and, in the final stages of the war, it held the key to the invasion of France. To Napoleon the failure of his in-theatre commanders to gain early control of the east coast was one of the principal reasons for the defeat of the *Grande Armée* and the loss of the war.

If the war on the east coast was truly joint, it was undoubtedly one of the best examples of combined, or coalition, warfare at the lower level of all the Napoleonic struggles. Although the battles, sieges and engagements, from the allied perspective, were not glaring successes, the fact that they took place at all owes great credit to many of the commanders at the tactical level. It also reinforces the undisputable fact that Wellington was an outstanding allied commander. His 'Memorandum for Operations on the East Coast' was but a fleeting example of his genius and judgment in this arena.

To Lieut, General Sir John Murray, Bart. 14th April, 1813.

MEMORANDUM ON THE OPERATIONS TO BE CARRIED ON, ON THE EASTERN COAST OF THE PENINSULA

1. It is obvious that these operations cannot be commenced with advantage, till the allied British and Portuguese army shall take the field in Castile, which is intended in the first days of the month of May.

2. The troops applicable to these operations are the allied British and Sicilian corps, and the Spanish divisions under Major General Whittingham and Major General Roche, under the command of Sir John Murray; that part of the second army under General Elio, composed of regular troops; and the regular troops of the third army under the command of the Duque del Parque.

3. The objects for the operations of the troops on the eastern coast of Spain are first to obtain possession of the open part of the kingdom of Valencia: secondly, to obtain an establishment on the sea coast north of the Ebro, so as to open a communication with the army of Catalonia; and eventually, thirdly, to oblige the enemy to retire from the Lower Ebro.

4. Although these objects are noticed in this order, circumstances may render expedient a departure from it, and that the one mentioned in the third instance should precede that mentioned in the second.

5. If Sir John Murray possesses the means of embarking 10,000 infantry and artillery, or more, the first and second objects may be combined with great advantage : that is to say, that the attempt to secure the second object by a brisk attack upon Tarragona with all the British and Sicilian corps, and such part of the division of General Whittingham or General Roche, as can be transported to Tarragona, will necessarily induce Suchet to weaken his force so considerably in Valencia, as to enable General Elio and the Duque del Parque to take possession of a great part, if not of all the open country in that kingdom.

6. The first object will then be attained.

7. The second will be a question of time and means. If Suchet, notwithstanding the junction of the troops of the first army with those under Sir John Murray, should be so strong in Catalonia as to oblige that general to raise the siege, and to embark without accomplishing his object, the first object will at least have been gained without difficulty; and the return of Sir John Murray's corps into the kingdom of Valencia will secure it.

8. If Sir John Murray should succeed in taking Tarragona, the first and second objects will have been attained, and a foundation will have been laid for the attainment of the third object.

9. Orders have been sent for the Duque del Parque to commence his movement from his position at Jaen, and to proceed to put himself in communication with the second army, either by posting himself at Almanza, or at Yecla.

10. As soon as the corps under the Duke del Parque arrives in communication with General Elio, the allied British and Sicilian corps, and General Whittingham's division

should embark, to the number of at least 10,000 men, or more if possible, and proceed immediately to the attack of Tarragona, in which they should be aided by the first army.

11. The troops remaining in the kingdom of Valencia, that is to say, those under the Duque del Parque and General Elio, and those of General Whittingham's and General Roche's divisions, and of the allied British and Sicilian corps which should not embark, should continue on the defensive, and retire, even upon the lines at Alicante, if it should be necessary.

12. But as soon as it shall be found that Suchet begins to weaken his force in the kingdom of Valencia, they are to follow him up, and take possession of as large a part of that kingdom as it may be in their power to do.

13. It must be understood, however, by the General Officers at the head of these troops, that the success of all our endeavours in the ensuing campaign will depend upon none of the corps being beaten, of which the operating armies will be composed; and that they will be in sufficient numbers to turn the enemy, rather than attack him in a strong position; and that I shall forgive any thing, excepting that one of the corps should be beaten or dispersed.

14. Sir John Murray will take with him to the siege of Tarragona such of the allied British and Sicilian cavalry as he may have horse transports to convey ; the remainder, with the cavalry belonging to General Whittingham's division, will remain with the troops under General Elio and the Duque del Parque.

15. If General Sir John Murray should be obliged to raise the siege of Tarragona, and embark, or, at all events, when he returns to the kingdom of Valencia, he is to land as far to the north as may be in his power, in order to join immediately on the right of the troops under General Elio and the Duque del Parque ; and the mules and other equipments belonging to the allied British and Sicilian corps, which must necessarily be left behind at Alicante, are to join that corps at the place of disembarkation.

16. If Tarragona should be taken, it must be garrisoned by a part of the first army under General Copons.

17. In case Sir John Murray should not have the means of embarking 10,000 infantry, at least, the corps of troops to undertake a serious operation on the sea coast in the rear of the enemy's left, will not be sufficient, and the plan must be altered; and the following measures must be adopted to obtain a sufficient force in rear of his right.

18. First, The regiments, as stated in the margin (Voluntarios de Jaen, of the first division of the second army; the regiment of Alicante, of General Roche's division; 2nd de Burgos, of General Whittingham's division) must be detached from the second and third armies, and must be embarked. These, with about the same number recently ordered from Galicia, will augment the army of Catalonia sufficiently to enable them, according to the opinion of General Copons, to take the field against the enemy's troops now in Catalonia, and to force them to remain in their garrisons.

19. As soon as he shall be joined by these reinforcements, General Copons should make himself master of the open country, particularly between Tarragona and Tortosa, and that place and Lerida.

20. Secondly, the third army of the Duque del Parque should be employed to turn the right of the enemy's positions in Valencia, while the allied troops under Sir John Murray and General Elio will attack them in front. I imagine that it will be necessary for the Duque del Parque to proceed, in this case, as far as Utiel and Requena, before he will be able to make any impression on the position of the Xucar.

21. In proportion as the allied troops shall gain ground, this operation will be repeated ; the third army continuing to move upon the enemy's right till it shall come in communication with the first army on the left of the Ebro. With this object in view, General Copons and the Duque del Parque should keep in constant communication.

Note. It would be very desirable that, if practicable, General Copons should get possession of Mequinenza.

22. When the enemy shall have been forced across the Ebro, either by the maritime operations in rear of his left, or by those just described on his right, it will rest with General Sir John Murray to determine, in the first instance, on the line to be pursued, in a view to the local situation of affairs, in respect to the ulterior objects of the operations; whether to establish the Spanish authority in the kingdom of Valencia, by obtaining possession of Murviedro, Peñiscola, and any other fortified posts there may be within that kingdom, or to attack Tortosa or Tarragona, supposing that that place should not have fallen by the maritime operations first proposed.

23. In my opinion, the decision on this point, as far as it depends upon the state of affairs on the eastern coast, will depend much upon the practicability and facility of communicating with the shipping on the coast, without having possession of the maritime posts in Valencia.

24. If that should be practicable, it would be most desirable to attain the second and third objects of the operations, without waiting to obtain possession of the posts within the kingdom of Valencia; respecting which, it is hoped, there would be no doubt, when the operations of the first army should be connected with those of the second and third, and of the troops under Sir John Murray.

25. The divisions composed of irregular troops attached to the second army, and commanded by Generals Duran and Villa Campa, should direct their attention to prevent all communication between the enemy's main army under the King in person, and that under Suchet.

26. The operations of these divisions should be carried on the left of, and in communication with, the Duque del Parque; and, in proportion as the third army should move towards the Ebro, the operations of these divisions should be pushed forwards likewise.

27. The division of Don Juan Martin must be kept in reserve, nearly in its present situation, and directions shall be sent to Don Juan Martin.

28. General Sir John Murray, having under his command the largest and most efficient body of troops, upon whose movements those of the others will depend essentially, will direct the operations of all the corps of troops referred to in this memorandum, when their operations shall be connected immediately with those of the corps of troops under his command.

29. If General Sir John Murray's allied British and Sicilian corps, and the whole or part of General Whittingham's division should embark, General the Duque del Parque will direct the operations ordered in this memorandum to be carried on in the kingdom of Valencia; but, in either case, the General Officers commanding the first, second, and third armies, and General Whittingham, must command each their separate corps.

WELLINGTON

Bibliography

Arcón Dominguez, José, Apuntaciones Sobre el Ejercito de Valencia en 1811, (Valencia, 2010).

Arcón Dominguez, José, Sagunto, La Batalla por Valencia, three volumes (Valencia, 2002- 2013).

Arcón Dominguez, La Batalla de Castalla 21 de julio de 1812, Desperta Ferro, Special Ed. #2.

Belmas, Jacques Vital. Journaux des sièges faits ou soutenus par les Français dans la péninsule, de 1807 à 1814, four volumes (Paris, 1836 -1837).

Durán de Porras, E., Inglaterra ante la Caída de Valencia: El Papel de Consul P. C. Tupper, Cuadernos del Bicentanario Number 13, December 2011.

Esdaile, C. J., The Peninsular War, A New History, (London, 2002).

Fortescue, J. W., A History of the British Army 1645- 1870, twenty volumes (London, 1899-1920).

Gómez de Arteche y Moro, J., Guerra de la Independencia, Historia Militar de España de 1808 a 1814, fourteen volumes (Madrid, 1868–1903).

Gómez Díaz, J., El general Contreras y el sitio de Tarragona, (Madrid, 2012).

Gurwood, J., The Dispatches of Field Marshal The Duke of Wellington, eight volumes (London 1844-1847).

Hall, Christopher, Wellington's Navy – Sea Power and the Peninsular War 1807-1814, (London, 2004).

Hugo, A., France Militaire, Histoire Des Armees Francaises de Terre et de Mer de 1792-1833, twenty volumes (Paris, 1837).

Lipscombe, N. J., The Atlas of the Peninsular War, (Oxford, 2010).

Lipscombe, N. J., Wellington's Guns (Oxford, 2013).

Oman, Sir C., A History of the Peninsular War, seven volumes (Oxford, 1902).

Muñoz Lorente, G., La Guerra de la Independencia en la Provincia de Alicante, (Alicante, 2003).

Reynaud, J. L., Contre-Guerilla en Espagne 1808-1814, (Paris, 1992).

Riley, J. P., Napoleon and the War of 1813, Lessons in Coalition Warfighting, (London, 2000).

Scott, T., The Diary of Major Thomas Scott RA (not published).

Suchet, Louis Gabriel, duc d'Albufera. Mémoires du maréchal Suchet, duc d'Albufera, sur ses campagnes en Espagne, depuis 1808 jusqu'en 1814, two volumes (London, 1829).

Thiers, M.A., Histoire du Consulat et de L'Empire, twenty volumes (Paris, 1845).

Ward, S. G. P. (ed.), The Diary of Lieutenant Robert Woollcombe, R.A. 1812-1813, published by the Journal of the Society for Army Historical Research, vol. LII, dated 1974.

Wellington, 2nd Duke, Supplementary Despatches, Correspondences and Memoranda of Field Marshal Arthur Duke of Wellington, fourteen volumes, (London, 1858-1872).

Whittingham, F. (ed.), A Memoir of the Services of Lieutenant General Sir Samuel Ford Whittingham, (London, 1868).

Zurita, R., Aliados Contra Suchet : El Apoyo Británico en el Frente este Español (1812), Cuadernos del Bicentanario Number 15, August 2012.

List of Maps

1.   The Siege of Tortosa ~ 16 December 1810 to 2 January 1811.

2.   The Siege of Tarragona ~ 4 May to 30 June 1811.

3.   The Siege of Saguntum ~ 23 September to 26 October 1811.

4.   The Battle of Saguntum ~ 25 October 1811.

5.   The (Second) Battle of Castalla ~ 13 April 1813.

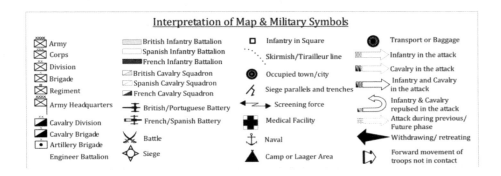

This work is dedicated to Marshal Suchet, undoubtedly one of Napoleon's most capable Peninsular Lieutenants.

Marshal Louis Gabriele Suchet, Duke of Albufera (1770-1826)

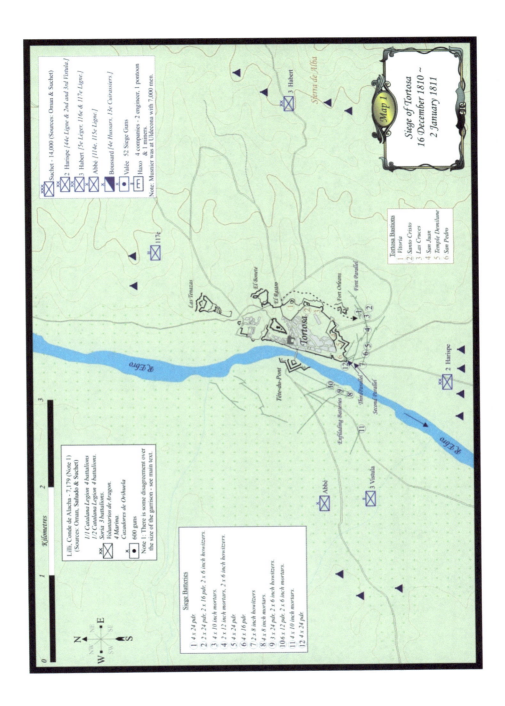

Map 1

Siege of Tortosa
16 December 1810 ~
2 January 1811

Suchet - 14,000 (Sources: Oman & Suchet)

2 Harispe [44e Ligne & 2nd and 3rd Vistula.]

3 Habert [5e Leger, 116e & 117e Ligne.]

Abbé [114e, 115e Ligne.]

Boussard [4e Hussars, 13e Curassiers.]

Valée   52 Siege Guns

Haxo   4 companies - 2 engineer, 1 pontoon & 1 miners.

Note: Musnier was at Uldecona with 7,000 men.

Tortosa Bastions
1 Vitoria
2 Santo Cristo
3 Las Cruces
4 San Juan
5 Temple Demilune
6 San Pedro

Siege Batteries

1 4 x 24 pdr.
2 2 x 24 pdr. 2 x 16 pdr. 2 x 6 inch howitzers.
3 4 x 10 inch mortars.
4 2 x 12 inch mortars. 2 x 6 inch howitzers.
5 4 x 24 pdr.
6 4 x 16 pdr.
7 2 x 8 inch howitzers
8 4 x 8 inch mortars
9 3 x 24 pdr. 2 x 6 inch howitzers.
10 6 x 12 pdr. 2 x 6 inch mortars.
11 4 x 10 inch mortars.
12 4 x 24 pdr.

Lilli, Conde de Alacha - 7,179 (Note 1)
(Sources: Oman, Sañudo & Suchet)

1/1 Catalana Legion 4 battalions
1/2 Catalana Legion 4 battalions.
Soria 3 battalions.
Voluntarios de Aragon.
4 Marina.
Cazadores de Orihuela

x   600 guns

Note 1: There is some disagreement over the size of the garrison - see main text.

N NE
NW
W   E
SW   SE
S

Kilometres
0   1   2   3

3 Habert

117e

Sierra de Alba

Las Tenazas

El Bonete

El Rastro

Fort Orleans

First Parallel

Tortosa

Tête-du-Pont

R. Ebro

Third Parallel

Second Parallel

Enfilading Batteries

2 Harispe

Abbé

3 Vistula

R. Ebro

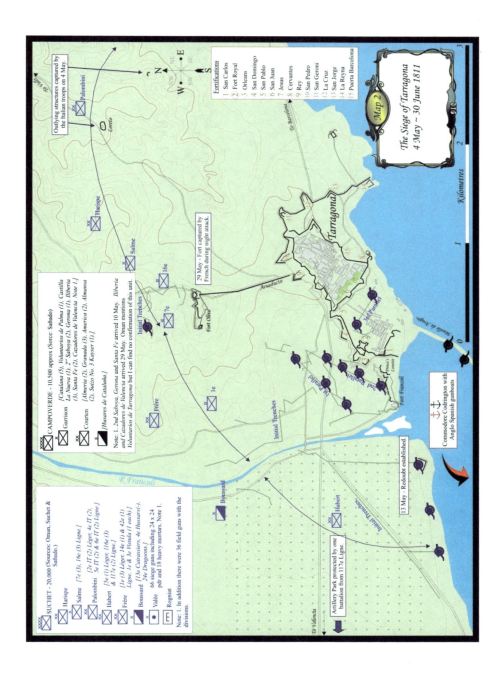

The Siege of Tarragona
4 May ~ 30 June 1811

Map 2

Fortifications
1. San Carlos
2. Fort Royal
3. Orleans
4. San Domingo
5. San Pablo
6. San Juan
7. Jesus
8. Cervantes
9. Rey
10. San Pedro
11. San Geroni
12. La Cruz
13. San Jorge
14. La Reyna
15. Puerta Barcelona

Outlying structures captured by the Italian troops on 4 May.

29 May - Fort captured by French during night attack.

13 May - Redoubt established.

Commodore Codrington with Anglo Spanish gunboats

Artillery Park protected by one battalion from 117e Ligne.

CAMPOVERDE - 10,500 approx (Sorce: Sañudo)

Garrison	[Catalana (5), Voluntarios de Palma (1), Castilla La Nueva (1), 3° Saboya (2), Gerona (1), Illberia (3), Santa Fe (2), Cazadores de Valencia Note 1.]
Courten	[Almeria (2), Granada (3), America (2), Almansa (2), Suizo No. 3 Kayser (1).]
	[Husaros de Cataluña.]

Note: 1. 2nd Saboya, Gerona and Santa Fe arrived 10 May. Illberia and Cazadores de Valencia arrived 29 May. Oman mentions Voluntarios de Tarragona but I can find no confirmation of this unit.

SUCHET - 20,000 (Sources: Oman, Suchet & Sañudo)

Harispe	
Salme	[7e (3), 16e (3) Ligne.]
Palombini	[2e IT (2) Leger, 4e IT (2), 5e IT (2) & 6e IT (2) Ligne.]
Habert	[5e (1) Leger, 116e (3) & 117e (2) Ligne.]
Frère	[1e (3) Leger, 14e (1) & 42e (1) Ligne, 1e & 3e Vistula (1 each).]
Boussard	[13e Cuirassiers, 4e Hussars(-), 24e Dragoons.]
Valée	
Rogniat	

Note: 1. In addition there were 36 field guns with the divisions.

66 siege guns including 24 x 24 pdr and 18 heavy mortars. Note 1.

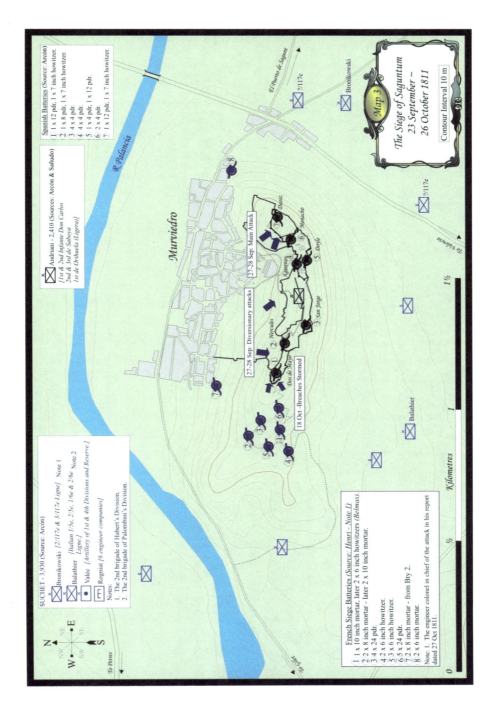

The Siege of Saguntum
23 September ~
26 October 1811

Map 3

Contour Interval 10 m

Spanish Batteries (Source: Arcón)
1 1 x 12 pdr., 1 x 7 inch howitzer.
2 1 x 8 pdr., 1 x 7 inch howitzer.
3 4 x 4 pdr.
4 4 x 4 pdr.
5 1 x 4 pdr., 1 x 12 pdr.
6 2 x 4 pdr.
7 1 x 12 pdr., 1 x 7 inch howitzer.

Andriani - 2,410 (Sources: Arcón & Sañudo)
[1st & 2nd Infante Don Carlos
2nd & 3rd de Sahoya
1st de Orihuela (Ligera)]

SUCHET - 3,930 (Source: Arcón)
Bronikowski [2/117e & 3/117e Ligne] Note 1
Balathier [Italian 1/5c, 2/5c, 1/6c & 2/6e Note 2
Ligne.]
Valée [Artillery of 1st & 4th Divisions and Reserve]
Rogniat [6 engineer companies]
Notes:
1. The 2nd brigade of Haber's Division.
2. The 2nd brigade of Palombini's Division.

French Siege Batteries (Source: Henri – Note 1)
1 1 x 10 inch mortar, later 2 x 6 inch howitzers (Belmas).
2 2 x 8 inch mortar - later 2 x 10 inch mortar.
3 4 x 24 pdr.
4 2 x 6 inch howitzer.
5 3 x 6 inch howitzer.
6 5 x 24 pdr.
7 2 x 8 inch mortar - from Bty 2.
8 2 x 6 inch mortar.
Note: 1. The engineer colonel in chief of the attack in his report
dated 27 Oct 1811.

27-28 Sep: Main Attack
27-28 Sep: Diversionary attacks
18 Oct - Breaches Stormed

Murviedro

R. Palancia

Duriel
Mauche
S. Doyle
San Jorge
Hercules
Dos de Mayo
Almenara

El Puerto de Sagunt
Bronikowski
7/117e
7/117e
To Valencia
Balathier

To Petres
To Gilas

N
NW NE
W E
SW SE
S

0   ½   1   1½
Kilometres

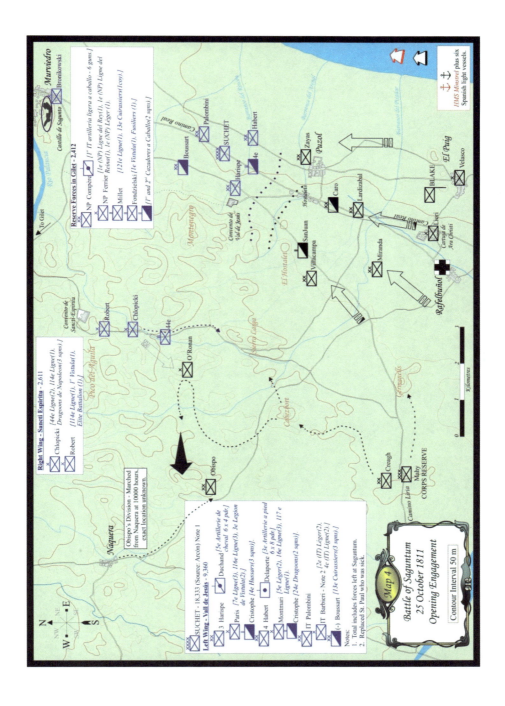

Battle of Saguntum
25 October 1811
Opening Engagement

Contour Interval 50 m

Map 4

101

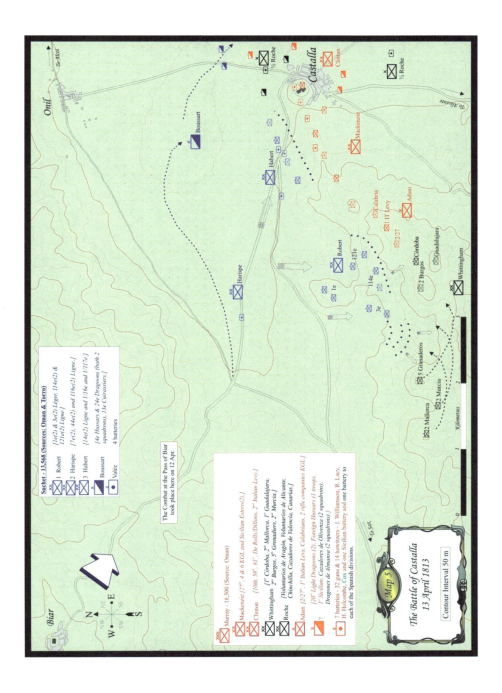

The Battle of Castalla
13 April 1813

Map 5

Contour Interval 50 m